T0339521

Cambridge Elements ≡

Elements in Histories of Emotions and the Senses
edited by
Jan Plamper
University of Limerick

LOVE IN CONTEMPORARY TECHNOCULTURE

Ania Malinowska
University of Silesia

CAMBRIDGE
UNIVERSITY PRESS

CAMBRIDGE
UNIVERSITY PRESS

University Printing House, Cambridge CB2 8BS, United Kingdom

One Liberty Plaza, 20th Floor, New York, NY 10006, USA

477 Williamstown Road, Port Melbourne, VIC 3207, Australia

314–321, 3rd Floor, Plot 3, Splendor Forum, Jasola District Centre,
New Delhi – 110025, India

103 Penang Road, #05–06/07, Visioncrest Commercial, Singapore 238467

Cambridge University Press is part of the University of Cambridge.

It furthers the University's mission by disseminating knowledge in the pursuit of
education, learning, and research at the highest international levels of excellence.

www.cambridge.org
Information on this title: www.cambridge.org/9781108813648
DOI: 10.1017/9781108884976

First published 2022

A catalogue record for this publication is available from the British Library.

ISBN 978-1-108-81364-8 Paperback
ISSN 2632-1068 (online)
ISSN 2632-105X (print)

Love in Contemporary Technoculture

Elements in Histories of Emotions and the Senses

DOI: 10.1017/9781108884976
First published online: February 2022

Ania Malinowska
University of Silesia

Author for correspondence: Ania Malinowska, a.h.malinowska@gmail.com

Abstract: This Element outlines the environments of loving in contemporary technoculture and explains the changes in the manner of feelings (including the experience of senses, spaces and temporalities) in technologically mediated relationships. Synchronic and retrospective in its approach, this Element defines affection (romance, companionship, intimacy etc.) in the reality marked by the material and affective "intangibility" that has emerged from the rise of digitalism and technological advancement. Analyzing the (re) constructions of intimacy, it describes our sensual and somatic experiences in conditions where the human body, believed to be extending itself by means of the media and technological devices, is in fact the extension of the media and their technologies. It is a study that outlines shifts and continuums in the "practices of togetherness" and which critically rereads late-modern paradigms of emotional and affective experiences, filling a gap in the existing critical approaches to technological and technologized love.

Keywords: love, technology, mediated emotions, cultures of feeling, mediated togetherness

ISBNs: 9781108813648 (PB), 9781108884976 (OC)
ISSNs: 2632-1068 (online), 2632-105X (print)

Contents

Swerve (Introduction)

What does it mean to love in technoculture? How is love conditioned in a technocratic environment, and is this environment an exclusively late-modern invention? This Element analyzes love and technology as they come together in hi-tech cultural contexts. Based on a premise that the question concerning technology is a question about love's apparent nature, this Element strives to understand love and its operational modes by understanding modern technological solutions for bonding. In *Love and Other Technologies. Retrofitting Eros for the Information Age*, Dominic Pettman sets up a critical model for rereading love as "technology of being together" (2006: 16). He observes that love, as performed in modern times, is an outcome of social industries and technological infrastructures that change over time. Love, he suggests, is an experience always already constructed. But what shapes our perception of and approaches to love is the swerve between "being" and "togetherness," distinct for a given moment of cultural evolution. This Element probes that swerve for late-modern societies.

Although technoculture has been around for a while, it is only in the contemporary moment – the past couple of decades – that our technological immersion has intensified into a radically different and game-changing form. My investigation into love-constructedness will be structured around (and indeed structured by) this new and singular moment. What I am specifically interested in is the sense of change around the way we love today. Is that change really as deep as we insist it to be, or is it just a different frame for what love has always been for us? The impact of automated environments on affective states is a fact. This fact brings to the fore the exoskeletal side of loving: love's increasingly advanced implements. Human "ascent" into *technosphere* – "the sum total of human technical achievements" (MacKinnon, 2021: 26), currently defined by digitization – redefines emotional interactions and their understanding, no doubt about that. But this redefinition also explains the technological nature of loving and clarifies reasons for why sensations are spoken of in terms of *techné*.

Love is many things. First, it is a feeling: an emotion, a state, an attitude, a reaction, an intra- and interpersonal relation. It is also a system of cultural significations: a tradition of expressing, justifying and legitimizing behaviors associated with the feeling of love. But first and foremost, love is a practice, a way of doing and cultivating whatever and however that feeling manifests. It hence entails a number of tools, techniques and instruments – or put broadly, *technologies* – that organize those manifestations and become love's second nature.

The correlation of love and technology has two sides. One is inscribed into the biology of bonding (and culture that follows): the Cupid's arrow effect, the increased dopamine level, love poems and the urge for affectionate expression, kissing, longing etc. This side reflects the instincts and praxes induced by the feeling of love and love agency. Pitirim Sorokin (1982) linked it with "the ways and power of love" and was the first one to explicitly consider love a technology. The other is infrastructural and concerns the social and material systems and facilities that emerge from civilizational advancement: the media, devices, machinery and equipment, anything we produce to refine our living condition and what our biology adopts and utilizes to make love happen. Both the correlations highlight the immanence of technology for the experience of love and the role of technological progression for affective cultures. In other words: there is no love without technology and love in itself is an essentially techno-logical occurrence.

And yet love and technology seem contradictory, almost antithetical. That conflict – invariably specious – intensifies as our in-real-life (IRL) routines disappear into cyberspace. Transferred to the digital plane, life as we know it loses its traditional tangibility. Our daily practices and activities, so far imbed-ded in the "solid" material reality, become estranged from their familiar settings and manners. Relationships look different, especially in how we carry them out. Encounters are less kinetic; conversations are less interactive. Hook-ups, which now abide by the strict protocols of dating apps, which push a fill-in-the-blank approach to person expression ("give us three words that describe you!") and whose UIs constrain the possible modes of interaction, are more about autopre-sentation (rather than exchange). Togetherness becomes technically and choreographically less reciprocal. Byung-Chul Han coined a phrase to reflect on the technology-ridden disinterest in the object of love, calling it "the corro-sion of the *Other*" (2017: 1). This, according to Han, is the essence of the demise of all affective engagements. And yet, modern technologies, despite their discord with the ethical and philosophical ideals of love, reanimate our affective relationships. They certainly make them more diverse, marking some new momentum. Although this novelty is often accused of deforming togetherness and distorting love's inherent paragons, there is a reformative aspect to it, one beyond technoenthusiasm and technoscepticism. "Novelty as deformation" defines love in technoculture. This also defines the role of technology for love across time.

As we progress into the future, the technology-inspired styles of companion-ship and intimacy become more a matter of a potential rather than quality (especially since it looks like social distancing will be in our future for some time). When COVID-19 put half of the globe under lockdown, transmission media took over most of our emotional (and other) interactions. The question of physicality or contact became unexpectedly urgent again. Not that they were new. For the first time in human history, traditional axioms of an encounter – that of the mode (face-to-face), locus (restaurant, hotel) and temporality (natural/analogue time; social time) – were almost completely replaced by their digital counterparts, and on a global scale. Although isolation will not become the norm – at least not for a while – remote contact and intimacy are being debated in terms of solutions for relationships and also in terms of the nature of feeling itself. Perhaps intimacy does not need proximity. It may not even need a body. To paraphrase Catalina L. Toma (2018), togetherness today seems to be a conflict of distance and connection. We want to love but without the presence of the other. Pandemic or not, relationships are increasingly more physically remote, as if we have opted for a fantasy lived on our own.

If the real-time body is no longer love's major game, what then makes this game still so irresistible, so appealing? As I probe into this query, Facebook is launching their first dating service based on connecting "people who like what you like." This matchmaking technique, invariably extreme in how it radicalizes the age-old trick of the commonality of preferences, again puts criterion (the affinity of taste) before experience (the actual encounter). It seems like love is the narrative of shared proclivities rather than shared time and space, the latter now kept in the "option" box. The techniques for distant closeness condition the hi-tech environment and thus condition love in this environment's setting. What interests me is how this situation possibly affects the distribution of feelings and how it impacts our understanding of love as an experience.

When I say love, I mean a union. Or, to be specific, I mean an affective emotion and state aimed at the formation of a relationship (be it a marriage, an affair, a companionship, or any other emotional or intimate engagement). Nozick (1989) defines this kind of love as the *desire* to form a "we," a desire that entails a striving for affectionate and intimate reciprocity. It might be between people, but also between people and technologically engendered subjects. Crucial to this reciprocity, however, is the intention and function of bonding. Therefore, the "love" described in the Element is less concerned with the philosophical ideal of loving (what love should or is expected to be). Instead, it focuses more on the actual practice of loving, that is, on "styles" of couple or companionship formation and what the formation practically entails in technoculture.

My use of the term "technoculture" connotes "the interdependence of technology and culture" (Shaw, 2008: 176). But to escape definitional generality, I narrow the term down to cultures inspired by the integration of hi-tech into social communication and changing communication standards. This sets my analysis in a specific context related more to the deployment of technology rather than actual geography. In this context (marked by technological development), technoculture is a peculiar token of modernity and a measure of civilizational advancement, both defined by access to latest technologies. It is perhaps wise at this point to say that, due to its defined conceptual approach, this Element focuses mostly on High Modern societies during the last two or three decades since the digital revolution. Although it makes occasional trips to the Early Modern Period, it concentrates on the contemporary times and on those parts of the global West and East where the practice of technology is comparable.[1] It does not discuss differences in such conditioned technological modernities (except for when it points to critical distinctions between cultural traditions of technology), just like is does not undertake differences in how technoculture and love are experienced by various minority groups. I treat technology as a unifying force that establishes a certain standard for the social practice that we hack and negotiate, yet nonetheless follow regardless. Though many of the examples used in this Element may play out differently in various social contexts (such as LGBTQI and others), I do not scrutinize them here, partly because more comprehensive and insightful studies do it much better. Furthermore, some of those studies express doubts that those differences actually exist or are sustainable (e.g. Lamont, 2017). Following Lelia Green (2002), I reserve the term "technoculture" for the use of "communication technologies [and hi-tech devices] used in the mediated construction of culture" (xxviii). I am therefore faithful to her conviction that technoculture transcends traditional senses of geography (by transcending the traditional senses of kinesis). This is the very condition of technology as a cultural occurrence.

> To be technocultural, [Green explains] the technology concerned must facilitate cultural communication across space and/or time and should, in some way, raise issues of place. Since culture is a construction involving communication, and more than one person, technoculture involves the communication of cultural material in technological contexts – which is to say, other than the face-to-face. If this definition were to be adopted, future discussions of

---

[1] A good reflection of my geographical assumptions is a GFluene's 2017 report on the global use of dating apps based on the BBC report carried out a year before (see: https://gfluence.com/people-find-love-global-overview-dating-apps/). The map included in the survey depicts the deployment of new communication media and therefore "defines" modern societies with regard to access to hi-tech (https://gfluence.com/wp-content/uploads/2021/02/Global-love-app-map.png). Of course, the proposed image does not give a reliable overview of the use of new technologies, as it is limited to communication media only. Nonetheless, it renders the understanding of geography covered under the term technoculture. At the same time, it is worth noting that a similar post-Covid report may give a slightly different view of the new media use (with active access to technologies being more extensive).

technoculture would indicate reference to a technology that allows the construction of culture across space and/or time. (xxviii)

I, nonetheless, approach the prefix *techno-* rather holistically. Technology is the
forces – manipulations and manifestations – by means of which humans anchor
themselves in the environment and by means of which they "naturally" (or
unnaturally) make the environment transform. To speak of technology is to
speak of technicity, technics, *techné* and techniques reflected in tools used for
the extension of "man" and the cultures such an extension creates. It is also to
speak of the tools extending themselves with man in the process of technological *poiesis*. Only in this way can we grasp the actuality of our technological
condition and understand the nature of phenomena traditionally considered
nontechnological, in this matter, love. As a technological occurrence, love is
a revelation of the modern *Gestell*. Just like the modern *Gestell* is the revelation
of possibilities for experiencing the occurrence of love. Modern technologies do
not change love. They unveil love's inherent technicity in how they extend the
experience of loving beyond the experience's expected nature.

Technology taps into love's hidden aspects and affordances, many of which
are so far repressed by the rule of decorum or simply physically unrealized.
When reality was still mostly analogue, love happened between people. Devices
were seen as auxiliary and nonintrusive. Nobody considered media a part of an
emotional and intimate exchange. Let alone its active participant. Now, with
"intelligent" media – the media that are more interactive and seemingly more
autonomous – the share of mediated emotions gets more complex. We become
as emotional about the devices that mediate our romantic (and other) relationships as we do about our romantic (and other) partners. What is more, the
devices themselves become objects of our affection, fantasy or desire. In
"Sensitive Media," Toby Miller and myself (2017) explain how "the sensitization of 'the media things' [has affected] the redefinition of our affective and
emotional experiences." Pointing to technological sentience, we probe the
condition in which a cell phone triggers emotions normally reserved for humans,
and in which Assistant AI (e.g. Siri) or companion robots are both a medium of
relationship and its immediate addressee. It turns out that our attachment to
technological objects, developed in daily interactions with and via the objects,
makes us think of those objects as objects that themselves "feel" (665). This is
how new technologies revolutionize our perception of the matter of bodies and
our thinking about an affective subject. Marie-Luise Angerer (2015) refers to
modern technologies as a *dispositif of affect*. Technological devices and protocols, she says, inspire affective environments whereby the human body is no
longer an ultimate definition of a feeling organism. In a strictly posthuman and

new materialist vein, Angerer reaffirms the liveliness of things, reminding us that emotion and its related affects are a preconscious, and most importantly, universal capacity. With this she supports theoretical voices which convincingly argue that feeling is not "an intrinsically organic occasion" (Pettman, 2018: 13). Those voices consider the existence of nonintentional sentience, a quality (or qualia) of both organisms and things (Shaviro, 2016: 18). Two paradigms that explain this situation best are Dominic Pettman's *Creaturely Love* and Mario Perniola's *Philosophical Cybersex*. Whereas the first one revisits the hierarchies of species' capability to feel, the other convinces that we are moving away from organic desire, and towards an artificial intimacy (and pleasure) that is beyond human aesthetic (and ontological) conditioning.

Pettman reviews human emotional supremacy in the animal kingdom. In this review, "the human is [no longer] an animal body blessed with a human soul – a kind of superanimal – but instead a bundle of physical, psychical, and sociological mechanisms, shot through with prehuman, inhuman, posthuman, and infrahuman tendencies and trajectories" (2017: x). Humans, therefore, do not hold a monopoly for loving, but they love by their specific criteria which coexist or are parallel to the criteria for love exhibited by other species. Perniola goes a step further and revisits human organicness. To him, people as surrounded by things become themselves the things that feel; as much as the things they surround themselves with become feeling subjects. Emotions happen by means of things and at their engagement. "It would seem" – Perniola writes – "that things and senses are no longer in conflict with one another but have struck an alliance thanks to which the detached abstraction and the unrestrained excitement are almost inseparable and are often indistinguishable" (2017: 1).

To reflect better on this condition, I have proposed the term *technofeelia* (Malinowska, 2019), which accommodates the conceptual and environmental conflicts that make us believe that the love we experience today is far from some original ideal of loving. *Technofeelia* – a pun-word to signify feeling-with-technologies – encompasses several transitions: towards a new phenomenology of psyche, towards a new experience of soma, towards new surroundings, landscapes and habitats, that, on the one hand, signal a tectonic shift in human emotional cultures (and how they are being organized) but, on the other, sees this shift as a continuation of a long tendency directed by humans striving to overcome their own biological reality and the physical reality of the world at hand. Love in contemporary techoculture, as defined by *technofeelia*, is the negotiation of the limits (and possibilities) for reformulating desire and redistributing affect, what these limits and possibilities mean, how they occur, and towards what they are evolving. It asks with whom and how exactly (or how differently) we desire to form a "we," and also how the "we" is actually being formed.

Deleuze and Guattari wrote about a "body without organs." They tried to render the situation of organisms, machines, objects and subjects in the state of constant becoming. Bodies, they claimed, transition between stages and forms, and are never static but always processual. Modifications that the body goes through do not so much depend on the body's organs as they depend on the entirety of the organs' interactions – internal and external – in the process of endless metamorphosis. Perhaps *technofeelia* would mean the state of emotional becoming whereby "feelings without organs" would defy love's conceptual predeterminism that defines love's experiential limits, ones we stay within or go beyond. Perhaps instead of shifts, we should discuss contemporary love in terms of constant transitions.

What should definitely be avoided in theorizing the experience of love is the distinction between "before" and "after technology." Such a distinction – prevalent in modern criticism – is as much inadequate as it is invalid. Already in Plato, desire is considered a technological occasion (Krzykawski, 2019: 42). Early modern accounts of love speak of it in terms of artifice and artisanry. The twelfth-century treatise *De Amore* reminds us that love carries within it a craft and technique defined by its very origin:

> [I]ts name (*amor*) [is] from the word hook (*amus*), which means "to capture" or "to be captured," for he who is in love is captured in the chains of desire and wishes to capture someone else with this hook. Just as a skillful fisherman tries to attract fishes by his bait and to capture them on his crooked hook, so the man who is captive of love tries to attract another person by his allurements and exerts all his efforts to unite two different hearts with an intangible bond, or if they are already united he tries to keep them. (Capellanus, 1969: 31)

But the hi-tech "hooks" we use now seem oddly less authentic. We seem to perceive modern love in terms of the *old* vs. *new* duality. Some incarnations of that duality – especially those of *natural* vs. *artificial* and *analogue* vs. *digital* – reinforce a conviction that the love we experience today is somehow unnatural and therefore wrong and not genuine. There is this tendency to eulogize the past way of life and deprecate the present. Far from idolizing our current moment and method (as for life as for love), there is a trap in thinking by means of caesuras and epochal markers. Change is a continuum and always reflects a tendency already inherent in objects or states. Our task is to see through the tendency's logic and learn its inclination. Only then do we understand its discontents.

Recent disappointments with the "event of love" are almost always related to the transfer of human interactions into the platforms we now tend to call reality.

Today's computerized control of *encounter* – that these platforms invariably allow – eliminates from the game of love the variant of contingency. In a shrewd criticism of online dating, Alain Badiou accuses the templates and protocols of virtual romance of enforcing the "zero risk policy." Dating platforms, Badiou observes, impose an impeccably accurate assessment of a potential match.

> This hype [he explains] reflects a safety-first concept of "love". It is love comprehensively insured against all risks: you will have love, but will have assessed the prospective relationship so thoroughly, will have selected your partner so carefully by searching online – by obtaining, of course, a photo, details of his or her tastes, date of birth, horoscope sign, etc. – and putting it all in the mix you can tell yourself: "This is a risk-free option!" ... Clearly, inasmuch as love is a pleasure almost everyone is looking for, the thing that gives meaning and intensity to almost everyone's life, I am convinced that love cannot be a gift given on the basis of a complete lack of risk. The Meetic [French online dating platform] approach reminds me of the propaganda of the American army when promoting the idea of "smart" bombs and "zero dead" wars. (2012: 7–8)

Badiou assumes that the informational optimization of risk causes a rift in the logic of love. Meticulous data collection, he argues, disturbs love's integrity, falsifying the process of affectionate bonding. But the datafication of encounter is not the problem here. The real issue is the nature of digital data. Information was once stationary, solid and slow. Now it is liquid, motile and extremely fast (cf. MacKinnon, 2021). It is also intensely multiple. According to recent estimates, we consume about 34 gigabytes of data and information per day. That includes an average of 100,000 words, read and heard in online and offline media. The standard for text messages is around 100 a day per person. It is more when we engage in "intense-interaction" platforms like dating sites. OKCupid delivers 2,500 match choices at the moment one signs up. Daily interaction is 10–40 or more matches, excluding likes and pokes from potential suitors. Such overdeterminedly designed "courtship" changes desire into reflex (we become reactional rather than responsive). And more importantly, it creates conditions of emotional precariousness, presenting (and thus defining) relationships as transient, ephemeral. The rules embedded in the design – rules which govern our practice of love in the digital space – shape the very *telos* of the love seeker.

In *Liquid Love* (2003), Zygmunt Bauman describes the frailty of human bonds as an effect of "the normatively established hierarchy of human value" (Best, 2019: 1096) and devaluation of desire. In his view, love has given in to the destructive power of the multiplicity of options. Eva Illouz (2011) later linked it with the "rationalization of passion" (16), calling modern romance a field of the constant evaluation of choice based on economic, aesthetic, political and emotional rationales. With the onset of the Internet, romance became the rapid flow of short-term estimations: of chances, choices and needs, additionally liquefied by the flow of templates, media formats and modes of interaction. This created circumstances of "complex immediacy."

> [G]etting sex now [Bauman observes] is "like ordering a pizza... now you can just go on line and order genitalia". Flirting or making passes are no longer needed, there is no need to work hard for a partner's approval, no need to lean over backwards in order to work hard for a partner's consent, to integrate oneself in his or her eyes, or to wait a long time, perhaps indefinitely, for all those efforts to bring fruit (quoted after Best, 2019: 1097)

The situation this passage is concerned with is much more complex, but I use it to illustrate the late-modern pessimism about the technocultural state of affairs (pun intended), according to which contemporary love is a corrupted and corruptive satisfaction-on-the-spot. The paradigm of *liquid love* tells us that human bonds are in a moment of a deep crisis. The reason for it is an almost complete commodification of intimacy, reflected in the automatization of the ways in which we satisfy desire. "Net delusion" (Morozov, 2011), which organizes that crisis, spurs the collapse of a very particular kind of social presence. Being more in touch, we are, at the same time, losing inter-human connection. The departure from face-to-face dialogue totalizes what the so-called transition media (e.g. telephone, telegraph) had only preluded. Social interactions – as they move ever deeper into cyberspace – become more anonymous, more elusive. If love is the "imaginary texture of the real" (Marleau-Ponty, 1964: 165), love in cyberspace is an imaginary hallucination. William Gibson, who linked cyberspace with consensual hallucinatory states, found that space deeply alienating. "The ultimate extension of the exclusion of daily life, [cyberspace, allows you to] literally wrap yourself in media and not have to see what's really going on around you?" (in Woolley, 1992: 121). But what when that space becomes *the* reality? What when it becomes *the* daily life?

Sherry Turkle (2011) once observed that while it is a huge disappointment, virtual space is also a space of huge expectations. "People talk about Web access ... 'as the place for hope' in life, the place where loneliness can be defeated. ... People are lonely. The network is seductive" (48). Togetherness – even if mediated or simulated – is an aphrodisiac. Online companionship satiates the emotional hungers we develop IRL. It is perhaps because most emotional processes happen in the brain. Psychology studies confirm that virtual relationships, because "they are conducted between flesh-and-blood people" are not "imaginary [but] a part of reality" (ben Ze'ev, 2008: 2), that is, they are experienced as real. While it is merely an incomplete solution, virtual contact does grant us some satisfaction and contentment. It makes us feel less lonely even if only for a while and only very superficially. The actual depth of online interactions cannot be measured, but there are new research projects that explore their benefits and potency. There are also voices arguing that "technology can help us reimagine and reinvent how we understand love and life ... without losing sight of one's self and of losing the sight of others" (Papacharissi, 2018).

In this Element, the late-modern critical scepticism about technologized love is revisited through an examination of the areas of reinvention: practices, cases, occurrences and technology-driven trends that design and reimagine the idea of companionship. Far from techno-enthusiasm, I look at the standards of mediated affection and analyze them by the prism of cultural and artistic criticism around contemporary "intimacy and emotion styles."

The first section, "Subjects (The Technologized Other)" refers to the emergence of *an artificial object of love*, and talks about human relationships with technological things, from hugging robots to love "avatars." The particular problem it breaks down is the idea of technological subjectivity – nowadays so widely discussed in the context of "sex robots" – and the programming of feelings that has emerged alongside affective computing. The section traces the transition from *fetish love* to *objectophilia* to analyze the human understanding of emotional exchange with regard to the affective potential of artificial love objects, their thingness and orientation.

The second section, "Spells (Cybernetics of Feeling)," examines the algorithmic construction of "the event of love." It explains love as a semiotic system based on codes intended to signify and evoke a given emotional response later translated into a specific social engagement and cultural function. It seems like contemporary relationship platforms and gadgets continue that which early modern love games encoded for the experience of love, turning the experience into a race for achievement encrypted with rules and procedures. It is my position that love is a code and that we are more willing to engage in the experience of the code of love rather than the experience of love itself.

The third section, "Scenes (Emotional Techno-Spatiality)," considers the problem of space and spatial dynamics with regard to love's digital and mediatized environment. Special attention is given here to the notion of presence and movement in relationships but also to the veracity of virtual reality as a milieu for togetherness. I look at what happens with the event of love after its gradual transfer into the virtual. My interest here is how the technosphere and its material environment has changed the spatial semiotics of intimacy and impacted the understanding of remoteness for emotional interaction.

The fourth section, "Soma (Intangible Extensions)," is inspired by the emergence of haptics and hologram technologies, and discusses the "obsolescence" of the human body as we know it. I discuss how the rise of hi-tech devices for mediating feelings and somatic experiences transforms the soma of love, but also how the body becomes an extension of the media, altering its somatic capacity. With this, I try to map the shift in the physical experience of loving, to see how the use of proxies or the investment into noncontact encounters has impacted emotional experiences and the physical makeup of emotional interactions. I try to answer whether the absence of physical presence for romantic/intimate relationships is indeed a "modern invention."

The fifth section, "Speeds (Affective Temporalities)," looks at the temporalities of love, and the characteristics which have emerged from the onset of the high-speed life environment. The term I employ here, *fast love*, defines the "temporal modes" of togetherness for modern-day societies as set against the previous "slow life" ideals. I investigate the relationship between social acceleration, modern technologies and current practices of love, with specific interest in how present-day practices of romantic intimacy contribute to the further acceleration of personal and social routines. My aim is to look into how the management of love and how it leans towards immediacy inspires the development of new technologies, and consequently how this perhaps stimulates new forms of amorous contexts. Specifically, this section traces the trajectory of change in distributing love codes and behaviors though social systems from analogue, temporal and calculable towards digital, ultra-rapid and computational.

The "(Post)Script (Conclusion)" presents a number of statements on the swerves in the experience of loving. It is provided in place of a conclusion, to leave an open ending to the claims that *Love in Contemporary Technoculture* dares to make.

1 Subjects (The Technologized Other)

A reliable feature of technologized love is a decrease in the interest that humans have in one another. Not only do we seem less inclined to engage with fellow humans, but we also seem to be finding pleasure in technological artefacts that, by emulating human features, redefine our understanding of subjecthood.

Associated with "libidinal atrophy," this tendency is linked with the progressing depression of desire (Han, 2017): a depression that results from obscuring the trajectories of a libidinal exchange, which no longer goes from self to another, but is "a One scene" (to paraphrase Badiou). According to Byung-Chul Han, "[l]ibido [today] is primarily invested in one's own subjectivity" (2017: 4). We engage with others – socially, emotionally, romantically and intimately – only as performing and achieving subjects subjugated to the enticement of a maximum gain at a minimal risk to our need for self-appreciation.

Human relationships no longer need another. To be precise, they no longer need the Other in Another: that is, a person (or personality) to frustrate the blunt sameness of the self, tailored by the templates of media technologies that codesign our interactions. Instead, we want a maintenance/reinforcement of the self in "fragmented . . . part-objects" (Han, 2017: 12).

This point gains additional weight when considered along with the idea of human emotional engagements with technological "subjects." Long exclusive to sci-fi imageries, those engagements are now emblematized by companion robots (Pepper), assistant software (Siri, Alexa) or holographic lovers. As part of the European Commission's initiative on artificial intelligence (AI), a project is currently being considered to grant smart machines "electronic personality." There has even been movement towards legalization of hybrid marriages. This trend has marked itself with people espousing animated characters on *bishōjo* (pretty girl) games (e.g. Love Plus) or dating devices (e.g. Gatebox). Two notable examples in recent decades were a man known as Sal19000 tying the knot with Nene Anegasaki (a virtual girlfriend in the Nintendo dating simulator) in 2009, and Akihiko Kondo, a Tokyan who married a Vocaloid anthropograph of cyber celebrity Hatsune Miku. The weddings, although they had no legal recognition, begot a new strand of objectophilia.

Prosthetic Intimacies

Infatuation with inanimate objects like buildings or statues is a long tradition with a short research record. Unlike sexual fetishism, objectophilia renders objects and structures into equal intimate and romantic partners, and is founded on a belief that objects have their own sentience. The ultimate objectophiles, those attracted to monuments (e.g. Eiffel Tower) or to musical instruments, claim to experience emotional reciprocity, as if the things they make out with had feelings. Many of them report a complete disinterest in human beings, finding intimacy with objects fully satisfying, both emotionally and sexually. Volkmar Sigusch (2008) terms objectophilia a form of neo-sexuality. He also views it as an effect of the ongoing commodification of human circumstances, stressing the relative commonness of this orientation vis-à-vis its alleged deviant nature.

As technologically supported objects become ever more animate, our idea of the body and a physical subject changes substantially. So does the idea of "animation." In this interesting time of digital automation, animation is no longer considered an organic capacity – one belonging to a living creature, or to a human – but one inherent to or achieved in objects which, when technologically "propped," turn into beings that "hover unsettlingly between states: neither dead nor alive, neither subject, nor object, neither human nor machine" (Bode, 2005: 8).

Anthropomorphic modelling also does the trick. The reconstruction of human physique in games and simulation platforms became a milestone in object sex. It is also what took technologically enhanced love to another level, inspiring a new age of agalmatophilia (attraction to statues, dolls, puppets or mannequins). A romance with and by means of digitally engendered characters is not a mere augmentation. It is a lifestyle and relationship model symptomatic of our changing perception of a love object, subjectivity and animatedness.

An insightful example of this is *Virtual Adultery and Cyberspace Love*, a BBC documentary about *Second Life* players. This millions-strong virtual community lives and loves vicariously through avatars fashioned after the users' most daring lifestyle desires. The avatars come as human characters or humanoid creatures. Interactions that happen in the simulation space unveil users' multiple fantasies with regard to looks, behaviors and routines. The avatars also enact different inclinations and different forms of appeal than those which the users are willing to manifest.

There are three variants of interactions in the simulation reality. First is the default avatar-to-avatar interaction, which means no cross-interest between the users and their avatars. In this variant, the users do not engage with each other's avatars nor do they interact directly with each other. The relationships take place between the avatars only, and are less role-playing and more fantasy-modelling. The second, user-to-user, variant assumes attraction between the users played out by means of the avatars. This sometimes results in IRL hookups or IRL marriages (circumstances permitting). The last, user-to-avatar, variant signifies the user's interest in another user's avatar and is emblematic of the so-called "Tamagotchi togetherness." This term is named after a Japanese digital pet in a handheld device that started a global virtual-care fad in the 1990s, Tamagotchi-simulated attachment and bonding between a child and an artificial companion, based on what Deleuze terms "positive distance" (1990: 172), and which signifies undemanding commitment. Intended for schoolchildren, Tamagotchi quickly caught on with adults, reinforcing the materially hybrid standard of loving.

The grown-up equivalent of Tamagotchi love is the Otaku culture represented by "men ... almost more likely to be dating an algorithm than a human being"

(Pettman, 2009: 190). First identified in 1983 as consumers of specific anime and manga, Otaku became known for their proclivity to hook up with animated or digital girls and develop strong psychosexual bonds with these technologically created characters. As such, the Otaku (a Japanese word for "nerd") perpetuate the ubiquitous and ever growing techno-animism associated with the onset of late-modern techno-intimacy. Their carnal affections for digital artefacts and images emblematize the ubiquitous techno-constructed reality, but also enact contemporary redefinitions of subjects, and their affects, as they reimagine the correlations between nature and culture. This is specifically true in relation to natural and artificial entities – their reimagining in terms of subjective experience (or what makes a subject/object feel and think).

But according to Yuji Stone (2014), Western readings of the Otaku practice connote too much sensationalism. These readings are notably especially oblivious of discrepancies between Western materialism and the Japanese understanding of interactions between humans, objects and their environments whereby all matter is affective by essence (and not by relations). In Stone's view, the "Otaku perversion" is a reflection of a specific cultural context rather than a universal fad. Unlike the Western obsession with virtual characters, the Otaku phenomenon reflects traditional thinking of ontologies embedded in Japanese socio-cultural infrastructure, in which objects are part of the environmental furniture as much as humans.

Despite these different motivations, techno-intimacy has kicked in globally. Its harbingers were early computer games (e.g. *Bachelor Party* 1982; *Leisure Suit Larry* 1987; *Sexi Paridius* 1996) and dating sims (e.g. *Girl's Garden* 1984; *Tokimeki Memorial* 1994; *Magical Date* 1996), which later grew with online life simulators (e.g. *Second Life* 2004), romantic/erotic subplots of role-playing games (e.g. *Baldur's Gate II* 2000; *Mass Effect* 2007; *Dragon Age* 2009), romance-oriented visual novels (e.g. *Love Plus* 2009; *Hatoful Boyfriend* 2011; *Mystic Messenger* 2016), and virtual-girlfriend apps for mobile devices. A vital addition to the latter are platform companions: online animated girls (e.g. Kari: karigirl.com) and boys (Invisible Boyfriend: invisibleboyfriend.com), or downloadable-as-software companions, and more recently portable devices featuring programmable partners, operated from a user's smartphone (Malinowska, 2020).

An unmistakable shift in prosthetic companionship came with the emergence of love robots. For decades relegated to fantasy (and fiction), they are now envisaged as potential spouses, lovers and friends – in literature and robotic design alike. Spectacular achievements in the latter, especially with respect to machine learning, have encouraged robotics-inspired branches of the sex industry, which markets hyper-realistic silicon sex-dolls (e.g. Harmony by RealDoll).

Although quite impressive in their performance (some of them are equipped with several personality programs), these love-robot prototypes are still very primitive and most certainly far from the desired ideal.

However, the fantasy keeps propelling the reality. According to robot love enthusiast and author David Levy (2008), "by around 2050 ... robots will be hugely attractive to humans as companions because of their many talents, senses, and capabilities" (21–22). Drawing on the trends in soft robotics – the most recent of which is promising "robots that will reproduce and ... then die" (Guillén, 2017) – Levy assures us that by the mid-century, robots will be advanced enough "to fall in love with humans and to make themselves romantically attractive and sexually desirable to humans" (22).

When Lyotard (1974) described libidinal materialism, the machine functioned as an anti-Oedipal metaphor for human complexity and man's struggle with cultural infrastructures. N-sexes was an idiom of one's libidinal idiosyncrasy and heterogeneity with which the human machines invested themselves into the social, also in an attempt to overcome epistemological or systemic restrictions for the body, organism and a social subject. When technological things – which we may most likely think of as the fourth sex – start to function as kin (citizens, companions, assistants, lovers), the machine-cohabitant gains a more literal sense (even if a human-robot marriage is still a vague horizon).

Intelligent machines are already distinguishing themselves with their artificial libidinal potential. It is not only an abstract matter of "technological personhood"; what is also at stake is artificial emotional and physical labor that raises questions about the role of technological objects (or subjects, maybe) for human desire. Lauren Berlant (2012), who defines desire as "the feeling one person has for something else" (8), points to the paradox of the feeling's two-way work. On the one hand, "it is a primary relay to individuated social identity, as in coupling, family, reproduction, and other sites of personal history"; on the other, "it is also the impulse that most destabilizes people, putting them into plots beyond their control as it joins diverse lives and makes situations." Desire, Berlant observes, "link[s] personal life to larger histories, [but] also measures fields of difference and distance." As such, "it both constructs and collapses distinctions between public and private: it reorganizes worlds" (13–14).

The question of how the clash of desires – that of the human and that of the machine – may recoordinate our social (and private) libidos with their environments is undoubtedly decisive. But what seems more vital is the recoordination of the drives that brought us to the clash of desires in the first place.

The urge to create a mechanical species is a famous topos of humanity. Attempts at artificial life are mentioned as early as the eighth century BCE, in the *Iliad*. The term "android" – "a robot in human form" – predates the later word "robot" by centuries, signifying "automaton with a human face" and an exceedingly human "enigmatic and unpredictable" desire (Kaplan, 2006: 155). In her analysis of "fetishism strategies," clinical psychologist Louise J. Kaplan observes that the pursuit of "mechanical humans" and, later, of intelligent machines lies in "fantasies, ... intellectual powers, emotional forces, and creative energies" (157) founded on a number of drives. "It seems," she argues, "that humans have a *hubris drive* that inspires them with the fantasy that they are able to breathe life into inanimate objects" (162). They "also have an *anthropomorphic drive* that motivates their fantasies that certain objects in the world around them are endowed with human characteristics" (161). Two more drives which determine the construction of technological subjects are the need for companionship (*social drive*) and interaction (*stimulation drive*). Both inspire the design of companion robots.

Pioneering in this field of inquiry were experiments in emotional robotics by MIT engineer Cynthia Breazeal. She created a "machine" able to engage affectively by "reading" and simulating human emotions. Kimset (the robot's name), was a construction equipped with a synthetic nervous system recreating the human need for socializing and stimuli. When neglected, it got bored, and would express its feelings by mimicking the behavior of bored humans (by sighing etc.). When left on its own, it expressed lonesomeness in a manner similar to humans (cf. Breazeal, 2002).

Kimset was an outcome of socially assistive robotics developed for the health care industry in response to a burgeoning insufficiency in the number of caregivers. It surpassed the provider function of previous therapeutic machines (PARO, Pepper) in the ability to interact reciprocally in emulating behaviors that engage human patients empathically. But as Kaplan observes, obsession with imbuing machines with human emotional intelligence under-mines "robotic intelligence"; it questions a robot's molecular potential, denying a robot's "own special vitalities and energies" (170). We are clearly still dealing with the so-called Pygmalion syndrome based on the imperative of affirming a human trait in an object by instilling into the object a replica of human DNA. What we thus seem to be seeking in artificial companions is a caring human – one that seems to be on the wane.

Interestingly, studies in human-robot therapeutic interactions counterbalance this view. They point to the growing interest in the robotic affect regardless of the human-made programming. Research in the elderly and children shows high awareness and appreciation of robots' affective idiosyncrasies. Patients in those groups perceive artificial assistants "as entities to interact with" rather than humans. Their acceptance factor is based not on seeking further appropriation (naturalization) but on the assistants' usability defined by the users' subjective needs and their individual understanding of a technological subject (Cavallaro et al., 2012). Also, the emotional investment in those interactions is genuine, and equals the investment in interactions with people. Despite many doubts about the veracity and value of technological companionship, our brains (and our hearts) seem to be taking it seriously and for real. As Pettman notes in relation to men dating holograms or other technologically generated digients:

> the men are aware that their "girlfriend" is a computer program, but this does not diminish the erotic charge and psychological impact of the text messages they receive in response to their SMS courtship. For just as a child cries at the death of their Tamagotchi pet, these men shed a tear when their advances are spurned, and the AI (artificial intelligence) architecture chooses to reject them. (2009: 190)

Ambient Sentience

Technologies we use today happen to be deceptive (they trigger genuine feelings but also dupe our emotional responses). They also happen to be increasingly sensitive, especially in how they respond to stimuli and emulate affect.

If the question "Can machines think?" (Turing, 1950: 433) organized cybernetics in the 1950s and the following decades, the aspiration that organizes it now (and almost without question) is the machine's ability to feel. Since the late 1990s, affective computing – "computing that relates to, arises from, or influences emotions" (Picard, 1995: 1) – has taken over IT and communication engineering. It emerged from a conviction that "computers are beginning to acquire the ability to express and recognize affect, and may soon be given the ability to 'have emotions'" (Picard, 1995: 1). With the affective turn in science and the burgeoning theories of emotional intelligence, followed by disinterest in a "cognitive ability" as a defining feature for humanness, machines' affective literacy became the Holy Grail of human ventures with technology.

Despite the growing sensitization of gadgets – from wearables (depression detectors, sex add-ons: Kiroo Onyx and Pearl) to operational systems (Siri, Alexa) – technological things are not themselves emotionally autonomous. In other words, "feeling" machines, although they can recognize and respond to our states, moods and feelings, or emulate human emotional states (like Kimset), do not themselves feel, at least not the way we expect them to. Emotional self-governance – one of the ultimate goals for computational sentience – being a matter of technological advancement, is something we may expect to see in the near future. A bigger challenge is emotional singularity, which, because it depends on the mode of programming, is something that neither time nor technological advancement may help us attain.

The problem of affective computing is its reliance on the human way of understanding emotions. We imbue the machines with what we know about emotional states and subordinate the entire emotional design of intelligent devices to the human protocols of emotional conduct. Limitations of this approach are twofold: first, it prioritizes the physical parameters of human feelings; and second, it undermines the machine's affective potency. Jane Bennett called that potency the "positive, productive power" of material things (2010: 1).

Our emotional dynamics with technological objects are almost entirely based on the expectation that the objects through (and with) which we feel will empathize in ways we consider familiar or legitimate. Alternatives (like artificial emotional intelligence) escape our consideration due to negligence, indifference or lack of imagination. Like with nonhuman organisms (animals, plants, slime mold), we assume that technological things do not have sentience of their own (whatever that sentience might be and look like). Nor do we believe that they show any ability to empathize in ways we could acknowledge, and find on par with our own. There is a lot of myopia around the physical nature of objects. We treat material things as "simple, self-identical substance" rather than atomically complex "active and articulated processes – experiences, or moments of feeling" (Shaviro, 2014: 3).

And yet, intelligent machines keep signalling their singular affective potential. The first known machine-induced affective state was probably the "uncanny valley" – identified by Masahiro Mori in 1970 as an attempt to describe an estrangement towards a robotic object caused by the sudden decrease in the object's ability to emulate the anthropomorphic feature.[2] The uncanny valley names a negative emotional pool activated in people in response to a humanoid that fails to render the likeness of a person. The more the machine diverts from the human behavioral standard, the more repulsed a person feels. It is not, however, an accumulative feeling; rather, it is a sudden affect between a person and a machine provoked by the realization that what (or who) we are dealing with is not, in fact, a human being but a technological creature with "no personality." Mori diagnosed the uncanny valley during his research on machinic prosthetics. He described

---

[2] An interesting response to early automata (especially to *tableaux mécaniques*) was "machine possession" recorded by several European psychiatric institutions of the late 1800s, whose patients complained about being visited or possessed by a moving machine. More of a disturbance than a feeling, it was considered an effect of fear by admiration or awe – a common reaction to burgeoning mechanically propelled contraptions at that time.

a deep sense of alienation experienced by people exposed to the prostheses' imitational fakeness. "One may say that the prosthetic hand has achieved a degree of resemblance to the human form, perhaps on a par with false teeth," wrote Mori. "However, when we realize the hand, which at first sight looked real, is in fact artificial, we experience an eerie sensation" (Mori, 2012: 99). Similar experiences have been reported in research on human-chatbot and human-humanoid robot interactions. As technologies prolifer-ate, the sense of alienation in interactions with anthropomorphized devices lessens (Ciechanowski et al., 2018). The estrangement, however, does not completely go away, as if the affinity between "them" and "us" were something inherently erroneous.

More recent studies consider machines' abilities beyond anthropomorphism (including programming). Glitches, malfunctions and operational idiosyncra-sies are more and more frequently considered manifestations of extra affor-dances or properties rather than dysfunctions. Also, more and more often we take into account the postmaterial (subatomic) quality and qualia of intelligent machines as factors that may contribute to cocreating our emotional environ-ment. Although the question "What is it like to feel like a robot?" is being asked mostly among speculative realist philosophers (see Shaviro, 2016), certain cognitive robotics research has begun to take into account "affective states of computers" (Shaviro, 2016: 51) when programming or testing robots' ambient intelligence. Some of this research has even started to consider those states a possible new standard of love.

In 2017, Hanson Robotics, Open Cog Foundation and the Institute for Noetic Sciences started "Loving AI." It is an experiment aimed at "enabling humanoid robots to interact with people in loving and compassionate ways to promote people's self-understanding and self-transcendence" (Goertzel et al., 2017: 2). The project's ultimate goal is to enable "humanoid robots and associated AI technologies to express unconditional love towards humans" (2). The central mechanism in this endeavor is a meditation program in which participants experience guided mindfulness from embodied AI. The android used for that purpose is Sophia – the Hanson Robotics artificial maverick – equipped with "personality content and cognitive, linguistic, perceptual and behavioural content . . ., supplied via the ChatScript dialogue authoring and control frame-work, the OpenCog Artificial General Intelligence engine, along with a number of specialized software tools and a newly developed OpenCog-based model of motivation and emotions" (2). Focused on human bonding with a robot through consciousness exercises, the project promotes loving and compassionate inter-actions between humans and intelligent machines, exploring the material poten-tial of a machine to facilitate new emotional states.

Approaches adopted in this experiment combine the human protocols of feeling and the affective affordances of the machine. This method allows modifications of the human content or input with a "robot factor" and any latency that this factor brings into play. While the experiment, of course, is concerned with practical technological issues and protocols, the inquiry is grounded in and emerges from the protocol of "Human Unconditional Love," defined by the project designers as "the benevolent desire that everyone – ourselves, others, and all that exists in the universe, reaches their greatest possible fulfilment, whatever that may prove to be" (Mossbridge and Goertzel, 2017). This, they believe, facilitates the emergence of AI which incorporates unconditional love and is willing "to operate in the state ... that has as its primary goal enhancing the wellbeing of all beings and benevolent ideas" (Mossbridge and Goertzel, 2017). Such AI will be able to induce benign emotional states. Therefore "[h]umans interacting with [Loving AI] are likely to feel increased unconditional love and will be more likely to take actions that support the wellbeing of themselves and others" (Mossbridge and Goertzel, 2017). As the creators promise, "an AI with Unconditional Love will be designed towards the AI actually feeling Unconditional Love, not just behaving as if it does" (Mossbridge & Goertzel, 2017). And by "designed" they mean generated from the interactive and situated development.[3]

Ben Goertzel believes this is a shift in human-robot emotional dynamics:

> I think there's something big here ... If I were to sum this up in a cosmic sort of way, I might say something like: Via the experience of going through 'mind/body knot-untying exercises' with an AI that sees them and accepts them, people feel a contact with the Unconditional Love that the universe as a whole feels for them .... It sounds a bit out there, but that's the qualitative impression I got from seeing some of these human subjects interact with Sophia while she was running the Loving AI software. In the best moments of these pilot studies, some of the people interacting with the robots got into it pretty deep; one of them even described it as a 'transcendent experience.' This is fascinating stuff. (Goertzel et al., 2017: 12)

The premise for the project resonates with Oliver Brabant's postmaterialist model of consciousness (Brabant, 2016) – the project's direct inspiration. In

---

[3] The project is founded on two definitions of unconditional love: "Human Unconditional Love: the benevolent desire that everyone – ourselves, others and all that exists in the universe – reaches their greatest possible fulfilment, whatever that may prove to be. This love is freely given, with no consideration of merit, with no strings attached, with no expectation of return, and it is a love that motivates supportive action in the one who loves"; and "Loving AI Unconditional Love: An AI operating in the state of unconditional love a Loving AI has as its primary goal enhancing the wellbeing of all beings and benevolent ideas. Humans interacting with an AI in this state are likely to feel increased unconditional love (i.e. the human form), and will be more likely to take actions that support the wellbeing of themselves and others" (Mossbridge and Goertzel, 2017).

this model, "mind and matter are not viewed as two interacting substances, but as *correlated projections* from a common ground located in the quantum world" (Brabant, 2016: 353). Brabant assumes that mind phenomena such as consciousness and sentience happen separately from the brain, and entail experiences from inside and outside the body. Like other psychophysic and postmaterialist studies, Brabant's model contends that interactions, sensations and cognitive states emerge from, and take place in, a common (subatomic) ground where the subliminal self gets anchored to latent reality. In this reality – Brabant argues, quoting physicist David Bohm – "mind and matter are not separate substances [but] different aspects of one whole and unbroken movement" (Brabant, 2016: 353). Drawing on this argument, as well as on the assumption that the human mind feeds as much on conscious facts as on subatomic stimuli and information from outside the physical brain, creators of Loving AI use the robot as a source of extra data able to diversify (if not improve) the experiential dynamics of human emotionality. They tap into what physicist Henry Stapp associated with the broader potentiality of matter and its inherent mechanisms (reactions, exchanges, outcomes) not envisaged (nor undermined) by classical physics (Brabant, 2016: 348).

The technological apparatus for this experiment is the software engines of OpenCog – a multiple input and open-source self-learning AI platform aimed at the development of Artificial General Intelligence. OpenCog is a "diverse assemblage of cognitive algorithms, each embodying their own innovations – but what makes the overall architecture powerful is its careful adherence to the principle of cognitive synergy" (OpenCog: website). The system imitates the architecture and mechanisms of the human brain "without imitating the details" to ensure idiosyncratic (AI-inspired) confluences of intelligent behaviors "including perception, action, cognition, learning, memory, creativity, socialization, language, self-modeling, etc." (OpenCog: website). Technologies used in the platform allow the simultaneous development of a variety of nodes and networks that influence one another in ways unrestricted by the background/preliminary coding. This strong reliance on latent processes and outcome help overcome both resource and conceptual limitations. Additionally, they help bridge the gap between deep learning algorithms and symbolic reasoning algorithms, unveiling the possibilities of AI.

The project marks a three-stage transition in interactive AI that goes from *deep learning* to *deep understanding* to *deep feeling*. Conceptually, it marks a movement from Narrow AI to Artificial General Intelligence to Artificial General Emotional Intelligence, and aims at robots' ability to model themselves for benevolent emotional exchanges, in a variety of circumstances. Such a strong focus on "positive" singularity is all the more intriguing as it obscures the function-based and task-oriented idea of AI. "Learning-for-feeling" over "learning-for-problem-solving" means a tremendous shift in our expectations around technological subjects. We are clearly reaching a moment when the realization that AI does not have the same experience as humans brings into question our pragmatic instinct. It is also a moment when our pragmatism is being overtaken by the need for an experiential alternative (and an affective one). Are we, indeed, this jaded by our own species?

Sensitivity of ever-ubiquitous smart machines has opened doors to new interactive sensibilities. Researchers of intelligent systems speak of *ambient intelligence* (AmI) to emphasize the responsive and adaptive quality of intelligent devices (Remagnino et al., 2005). As technologies merge with the landscapes of our lives and living, they show a better recognition of our needs. But our expectations are bigger than that of mere responsive functions. We want more than "electronic butlers" able to sense features of our environments. Our current interest is in artificial emotional literacy – one that shapes our emotional discourses and take us beyond our familiar and cognitively produced systems of emotional, intimate and amorous exchanges.

With artificial ambience as our new technological reality, we hope for "machines" that are sentient rather than intelligent. The ultimate aspiration is a new "system of feeling." Human emotional patterns – although so stubbornly recreated in the sentient AI design – are clearly on the wane or at least no longer sustainable in our encounters with smart machines. Moreover, a perennial question revives with new inventions. Each time a smart gadget pops up, we ask again: Can those things feel? And further, what would it be like to (co)sensitize with them?

Our interest in feeling technologies is purely strategic. As a species set on survival, we search for conditions (often through hacking and ever-refining our existing civilizational achievements) that ensure our continued existence. Seeking what is best for us, we either create means for dealing with a problem or eliminate the problem (often wrongly identifying the problem's connection to our wellbeing). Interestingly enough, this evolutionary solutionism also applies to our fellow species. For reasons yet to be explored, human contact is on the wane. Investments into mediated communication and hi-tech prostheses reveal that the "physical immediacy" of our own kind is an inconvenience. Our desire, never modern (to paraphrase Latour), eschews the human element. We strangely endanger one another's consistency.

Sartre believed that "hell is other people." What he meant was the torment of being obscured by the gaze – opinion, presence – of another. To be "transcended by the transcendence of another" was for Sartre an attack on the sovereignty of the self. Nowadays, when the self is sovereign in terms of the "display of its status," the gaze and its induced opinions are in high demand. Presence, on the other hand, is somewhat less at a premium.

When the outbreak of COVID-19 stranded millions of people in their homes, divorce and break-up rates skyrocketed globally. Big spikes were also noted in online dating subscriptions, by people who were loathe to meet in person during the interpandemic period. Nonpresence, especially for romance, became a specter of a new relationship standard. All of a sudden, human company (and companionship) – once desired (or at least tolerable) – is now a source of ennui and energetic depletion.

Energolatria – the cult of energy – which Frederico "Bifo" Berardi (2017) believes to define the entirety of our modern condition, has long excluded exhaustion as a driving force for self-preservation. Cultural theory situates exhaustion against libidinal investment: exactly on the side of annihilation opposing vitalism. Negative companionship (my neologism for the exhaustion with human proximity and presence), is the exhaustion in-between: the intra-stage in the trajectory of energetic depletion. Aware of our sapping powers, we realize that: "We do not want to be active." At least not reciprocally.

The reason to seek togetherness with digital "subjects" is the energy-saving passivity those relationships ensure. Despite the common claim, "alone together" (Turkle, 2011) is not a social standard; it is "together alone." Companionship and coupledom want to be a one-scene, which entails the entire new economy of the "we" and an entirely different libidinal intensity.

Hybrid relationships leave us with many dilemmas. On the one hand, they purport to resolve the problems of structured relationships by awakening the social functions of marriage, reproduction and gender. Many see them as a chance for togetherness beyond the socially and culturally sanctioned markers of eligibility. If Eros (to quote Byung-Chul Han again) "is the relationship situated beyond achievement, performance, and ability" (11), then "Tamagotchi for adults" seems like a climactic form of the erotic ideal. On the other hand, however, the design and marketing of those relationships kill every glimpse of hope for that ideal. Its first templates in movies and fiction left promises. When Rachel and Deckard of *Blade Runner* (1982) left together towards the end of the film, we hoped with anticipation: "Will they invent another kind of love relationship? Other scenes? Other myths? We [knew] nothing but this [did] not prevent us from dreaming of something beyond the Ulysses/Penelope couple and their *all too human* love" (Guattari and Rolnik, 2007: 425).

2 Spells (Cybernetics of Feeling)

Another question for the technologically bounded environments of feeling concerns love's actual pleasures and vehicles. What is the magic of bonds and relations distanced by devices and communication templates? What do we seek in the technologically saturated formats of cohabitation and what do we hope to satisfy? Judging by how data formation and the exchange of messages have changed in the past couple of decades – let alone changes in the written word (which is still a major player for the language of amorous confession and a new major player for intimacy due to sexting) – love spells, including "I love you," seem to be gaining a new significance and entering a new dimension. And yet, in the "Postscript" to *The Name of the Rose*, Umberto Eco suggests that "I love you" – that almost ancient, sacred and undoubtedly magical line for amorous confession – has lost its inherent charm. "A [postmodern] man who loves a . . . woman . . . knows that he cannot say to her 'I love you madly', because he knows that she knows (and that she knows he knows) that these words have already been written by Barbara Cartland" (1994: 67).

Quite aptly, and despite all skepticism, Eco places discourse in the center of love mechanics wherein "I love you" is not merely a gesture of a romantic disclosure, but a technic of feeling and a part of a large analogue code that (in the sphere of technologically bounded relations) comprises the primary purpose and pleasure in love. The three-word spell is as much a declaration of feeling as it is a system of signification we have learned to recognize. "I love you," Ackerman et al. observe, "represents a commitment to future behavior" but also "a desire to segue from short-term fling status to a more serious, long-term relationship, reveal[ing] a complex web of intentions and perceptions" (2011: 1079). If the heart ("the organ first used to define the term automatic") represents love (MacKinnon, 2018: 23), then "I love you" works as a signifier for the automated (encoded) expression we link with a feeling by means of language. Romantics doubted verbal and visual renditions of love, dubbing them an aesthetic mirage of the experiential. Modern poets concur, deeming the amorous and the intimate as incommunicable respective to feeling. And yet, language (verbal, textual or visual) works a major charm – no matter how inadequate; "words of love can enliven the blood and make the heart race, or cause the stomach to churn, the senses to sharpen" (MacKinnon et al., 2018: 1).

Algorithmic Discourses

Technology taps deeply into that "visceral" potency of language. What is mediation after all if not life idioms transmitted over distance? As the physical body disappears from communication, words (*the texted, the messaged, the emailed*) take over the contact, becoming the major catalyst of our embodied reactions. Technologies for love and intimacy expose this situation all the more as they operate within semantics traditionally associated with the physical (touching, kissing, talking etc.). Thanks to hi-tech devices and gadgets, we notice that relationships are mostly the vocabulary of togetherness deployed in (and within) the social. This becomes quite vivid when the isolation of the body totalizes language to the point where words supplant the body in the traditional sense, a quality exemplified in gadgets like Gatebox. Designed by Japanese Vinclu in 2016, this relationship device the size of a shoebox and the shape of a capsule sells an intelligent voice system under the guise of a holographic manga girl to bond with you and keep you company. Equipped with high-intensity projection, speech recognition and wireless technologies, Gatebox connects with smartphones and intelligent household systems to operate them interactively with an almost-human likeness. The gadget has been intended for "lonely salary men" whose rate in Japan reaches over 40 percent and whose interest in real women declines due to economic concerns. In the country where manga is as much a part of cultural tradition as it is a daily imaginary, to live with "your favorite character" that "will always do all she can just for the owner" (Gatebox, 2016) is a tempting and convenient prospect; their commercial is very convincing. As seen in the following script – an extract from promo footage – "the appeal lies in the intimacy of small talk suffused with a flirtatious desire to be close to the user," which we may dub "a small talk for maximum pleasure":

Device:	Come home early . . .
User:	(*texts back from his office*) It's only noon.
D:	Hmmmmm . . .
U:	I am heading home now (*he texts upon leaving his office*).
D:	Yaaay!
U:	(*on the bus*) I'm home soon.
D:	Can't wait to see you (*the lights in the apartment turn on*).
U:	In 10 min.
D:	I'll be waiting.
(*the moment he enters home*): D:	Missed you darling!

Gatebox sees "loving" as care and flirtation protocols enacted reciprocally for the re-creation of conditions traditionally linked with romance or companionship. Perhaps this is what togetherness and its related intimacies are after all: a set of "familiar courting rituals . . . connecting directly to the imagination – the phantasmic center of the libido" (Pettman, 2017b: 10–11)? Studies in phone sex, and most recently in sexting, suggest that our romantic and erotic encounters are organized by *scripts*: rules deployed by language that organize our sexual/amorous conduct (Simon and Gagnon, 1986). Garcia et al. (2012)

explain that intimacy or romance scripts "dictate behaviors, such as who does what and when in context" (166). They also dictate who says what with what effect on the interaction, and its extended reality (e.g. a date follow-up), particularly in gender-normative relations.

Spike Jones contemplates this in his 2013 movie *Her*. Far from a personal favorite, the film's plot provides a parable of love's discursivity. Theodore Twombly, a divorcee in his early forties, becomes enamored with a "female" operating system, Samantha. Accessed from a multifunctional cellular device, the system manifests its presence simply with a voice and a name on the display. Samantha, who clearly transcends the parameters of traditional physicality, is nonetheless able to trigger emotional bonding and erotic experiences. Conversational at the core and platonic at the start, the relationship between Theodore and his bot evolves into a full-fledged affair. Each stage of this evolvement is vocalized/verbalized and enacted by means of apt phraseologies. As the relationship moves from friendship to foreplay, the narrative and the idiomatically structured nature of emotions and their related affects becomes more and more evident (cf. Malinowska, 2018). One conversation reveals it this particularly well.

THEODORE: If you were in this room with me, right now, I would put my
                      arms around you. I would touch you.
SAMANTHA: How would you touch me?
THEODORE: I would touch you on your face – just the tips of my fingers.
                      I would put my cheek against your cheek . . .
SAMANTHA: That's amazing. . . . Would you kiss me?
THEODORE: I would . . . I would take your head into my hands . . .
SAMANTHA: Keep talking.

When analyzed in terms of interaction and content, love is just a game of codes. As practiced in society, love is, after all, specific vocabulary, gestures and cultural idioms that, because they have accumulated through the traditions of courtship, have created the intimacy protocols we associate with specific feelings or feeling-inspired behaviors. Repetition is key to the game, and links with the pleasure of recursion similar to that of addiction or habit. Christian and Griffiths (2016) associate it with "anticipating the anticipation of others" reflected in the exchange of emotionally charged statements: "'I love you,' says one lover to another; 'I love you, too,' the other replies." Barthes speaks of love-as-a-game-of-discursive-codes when writing about "lover's plotting" from fragments of language. Those fragments, recognized in all that "has been read, heard, felt" (4), reflect a "printout of a code" or "the image-repertoire" (149), which Dominic Pettman (2006) compares to "the world data bank of images of love, with which we construct our own imaginative mise-en-scenes" (20). "The lover," he says, "is [always] at the mercy of the code's signifying system ... designed in order to execute a program ... inscribed into society, in order to keep things running" (20, 30). "I love you" is therefore nothing but automatic articulation that organizes human feelings and relations across modern social systems.

In *Love as Passion. The Codification of Intimacy* (1986), Niklas Luhmann terms love a "generalized symbolic medium of communication" that helps align the personal libidinal instinct with public interest.

> [L]ove ... is not itself a feeling, but rather a code of communication, according to the rules of which one can express, form and simulate feelings, deny them, impute them to others, and be prepared to face up to all the consequences which enacting such a communication may bring with it. As early as the seventeenth century, people were fully aware of the fact that ... despite all the emphasis on love as passion, they were dealing with a model of behaviour that could be acted out and which one had in full view before embarking on the search for love. (20)

These models of behavior are now being transferred onto technologies. Adapted for a technological context, they also belie the common conviction that computer science patternizes the experience of love. Computer science merely reveals the pattern-line structure of our emotional interactions. It also shows the computationality and calculability of our engagements. Pavlo Shopin considers love a perfect resonance of algorithmic culture. As he observes, "love has given fertile ground for algorithmic solutions and optimization procedures" (2017). He also adds that "a nuanced, mathematically inspired look at romance reveals that there are calculable issues and quantifiable outcomes" (2017). The calculability of emotions and emotional expression is widely used in hook-up apps and platforms that use "affect parameters" for match estimations. It is also the foundation of flirtation chat-bots known for their reliance on linguistic coding and discursive permutations.

Since early cybernetics, affective patterns have been key in optimizing human-computer interactions. They have also been key in understanding the nature of human emotions for future design of intelligent machines. At the beginning, the idea was to prove the superiority of human intelligence over heuristic programming. It was also to show that emotions, no matter how well translated into code, could not attain the same level of sentient literacy and fluidity as they do in humans. A prototype for these experiments was ELIZA (1964–6) – an interactive computer program inspired by Rogerian psychotherapy. The choice of verbal models at that time was a direct result of the fascination with the efficiency of therapeutic approaches that maximized emotional input and affective engagement of an individual. The Carl Roger interlocution model was an interaction miniature with a "strong predilection for reflective responses, with a concomitant lack of responses in all other categories" against "passive acceptance, structuring, interpretation, and possibly reassurance" common to other psychoanalytical methods (Strupp, 1955: abstract). Fashioned after that model, ELIZA was able to emulate the illusion of conversation and its related affects, using conversational patterns and synthesized speech. ELIZA simulated and stimulated emotional responses through time-sharing and texting software. Her interlocutors typed the replies into the chat window and received replies in the same way. The replies tested high for Turing qualification, especially in terms of communicating sentience. Here is an example of an ELIZA-User interaction described by Joseph Weizenbaum who, as the system's creator, believed in the possibility of depicting and re-creating "a model of certain aspects of reality" based on expression (2021: 273):

[ELIZA:]   WHAT IS TROUBLING YOU
[User:]   Men are all alike.
[ELIZA:]   IN WHAT WAY
[User:]   They're always bugging us about something or other.
[ELIZA:]   CAN YOU THINK OF A SPECIFIC EXAMPLE
[User:]   Well, my boyfriend made me come here.
[ELIZA:]   YOUR BOYFRIEND MADE YOU COME HERE
[User:]   He says I'm depressed much of the time.
[ELIZA:]   I AM SORRY TO HEAR YOU ARE DEPRESSED
[User:]   It's true. I am unhappy.
[ELIZA:]   DO YOU THINK COMING HERE WILL HELP YOU NOT TO BE UNHAPPY
[User:]   I need some help, that much seems certain.
[ELIZA:]   WHAT WOULD IT MEAN TO YOU IF YOU GOT SOME HELP
[User:]   Perhaps I could learn to get along with my mother.
[ELIZA:]   TELL ME MORE ABOUT YOUR FAMILY
[User:]   My mother takes care of me.
[ELIZA:]   WHO ELSE IN YOUR FAMILY TAKES CARE OF YOU
[User:]   My father.
[ELIZA:]   YOUR FATHER
[User:]   You are like my father in some ways.
[ELIZA:]   WHAT RESEMBLANCE DO YOU SEE
[User:]   You are not very aggressive but I think you don't want me to notice that.

[ELIZA:]   WHAT MAKES YOU THINK I AM NOT VERY AGGRESSIVE
[User:]   You don't argue with me.

Weizenbaum wrote the ELIZA program to prove the limitations of a machine's communication skills. Part of his aim was to cool down the fantasies of hybrid cohabitation based on the popular premise that machines might become capable of emulating the human manners and mannerisms. Several problems he identified in ELIZA pointed to basic and serious interactive "incompetence" on the part of the machine. Among them were troubles with "(1) the identification of key words, (2) the discovery of minimal context, (3) the choice of appropriate transformations, (4) generation of responses in the absence of key words, and (5) the provision of an editing capability of [the system's] 'scripts'" (Weizenbaum, 2021: 272).

Weizenbaum considered intentionality and reflexivity to be major modifiers of meaningful interactions. He also found them exclusive to people and to human relations, and therefore impossible to recreate in a machine. ELIZA's merely rudimentary ability to imitate speech patterns was taken as evidence of the inimitable complexity of human communication. It also discredited the belief that humans can have empathic, meaningful and interactively genuine exchanges with intelligent machines. To Weizenbaum's surprise, however, ELIZA's interlocutors reported a high emotional engagement when in conversation with the program. Almost all the computer's interviewees spoke of a certain "psychological utility" of ELIZA's script that gave them the "sense of being heard and understood" (Weizenbaum, 2021: 272). A particularly interesting case was Weizenbaum's secretary, who in the first round of the experiment demanded time alone with ELIZA out of fear that their conversation was being eavesdropped on, as if ELIZA was a person capable of more than mirroring pattern-bound responses. The pattern itself – its repetitiveness and echo-like nature – was in no way a hindrance to a rapport. ELIZA's interlocutors seemed to enjoy the circumstances which (like in human-to-human conversations) allowed for "certain (perhaps generous) assumptions about [their] conversational partner" (Weizenbaum, 2021: 273). Those assumptions, Weizenbaum observes, "give way to conversational affirmations that create the impression of interest and engagement that the speaker further defends by attributing to his [or her] conversational partner all sorts of background knowledge, insights, and reasoning ability [which] manifest themselves inferentially in interpretations he makes of the offered responses" (Weizenbaum, 2021: 276).

Perhaps what ELIZA unraveled was not the superficiality of a computer's conversational skills, but the structuredness of human interactions, wherein intentionality and reflexivity are of much less importance than the appreciation derived from semiotic codes reflected in language. Perhaps the delight of human conversation is in the exchange of familiar patterns – phrases, gestures – which we ascribe to certain affects (or "affective states" such as love). Even if affect is largely regarded as prepersonal, preverbal, precognitive and preconditional, it binds together personal, verbal, cognitive and condition-ridden contexts. These contexts trigger codes that in turn trigger feelings (understood as personal affects) and emotions (understood as social affects) that immerse us in affective states (like "romantic love") whose outcomes are as much already framed as they are desired. Affective relations are therefore automated – algorithmic – "speech" for a specific purpose whereby "speech" euphemistically renders a script (of verbal and body language) employed to communicate feelings, emotions and intent.

Game Texts

Love algorithms have been with us since early modernity. "Medieval love" (commonly known as "courtly love," termed thusly after the court culture it emerged from) relied on a vast "technology" of words, looks and gestures, anchored in protocols that prescribed proper amorous decorum. "The Bible" (writes John Stevens in his depiction of courtly love) "did not tell a man whether he might pare his nails at table, kiss a lady when he met her, or write a love-song."

> It told him of his salvation, of his duties and responsibilities, of the spirit in which he should work and pray. Courtly love, on the other hand, was a gospel of leisure and pleasure. It taught you how to behave to your peers when you all had time on your hand; not how to do them good, but how to make yourself desirable; how to 'commune', especially mixed company, and how to please." (1979: 1955)

Those protocols came in the form of the so-called "game-texts" (Patterson, 2015) or "games of love" (Stevens, 1979), inscribed into long poems from fathers and mothers of early literature (e.g. Chaucer, Wace and Marie de France) who "dramatized" the practice of loving as much for the purpose of courtly entertainment as for moral wellbeing. The boundaries between "friendship" and "concupiscence" were very obscure in the courtly society of the late Middle Ages. What made them so was the flamboyant manner of that society, whose gestures "were more expansive, [and] rituals more overly elaborate" (Green, 1979: 201). "Game-texts" provided "the medium of polite intercourse between the sexes" that turned wooing into a role-play that "depended for its effect on an esoteric knowledge of acceptable forms [whose], inevitable moral ambiguity was, however, compounded by its heavy dependence upon formulae drawn from the metaphorical language of erotic verse" (Green, 1979: 202).

Affection games were usually the texual games of chance aimed at playful divinations used for the estimation of chances, as in love as in life (Patterson, 2015). They relied on copying amorous stanzas onto parchment that the players – both men and women – later exchanged in interactions, provoking a variety of "luf-talkying," reflected in "maxims and aphorisms ... riddles and jokes ... 'theme(s)', 'questions' concerning love ... debate(s) of a 'contentation'... talking-games, and so on" (Stevenson, 1979: 161). Notable examples of courtly amorous games were poems such as "The Parliament of Fowels," "Lays" and "Roman de Brut." Others were *Le Jeu d'Aventure* [the Game of Chance] and *Le Jeu d'Amour* [The Game of Love] (Patterson, 2015: 81), inspired by debate games also popular at that time.

The game-texts encouraged the mechanics of collective improvisations. This allowed romance to be an aesthetically stylized hunt in code-controlled circumstances wherein the script "was fine opportunity for dalliance" (Stevens, 1979: 157). The game participants were not simply persons but players who acted the Lovers. Romance, Serina Patterson observes, was about being immersed in the imaginary world wherein the players "may have enjoyed the display of etiquette and social mannerisms" (2015: 83). The romantic love we know today emerged from enacting the imagery of affection and intimacy that both rested on and generated codes of romantic conduct. The scripts to navigate that conduct defined the nature, mode and stages of love interactions, offering the reservoir of semantics (gestures, mimics and phrases) that the Lovers could contextualize in accordance with the code.

The same mechanics of amorous interactions lives on in modern-day affection games. Lindsay D. Grace, author and editor of *Love and Electronic Affection* (2020), explains that flirting and hook-ups in computer games undergo special modeling that are subject to the regime of "accepted" love codes and algorithms of conduct (e.g. algorithm of consent) that prescribes romance for the intended interaction. This is to offer players the familiar "settings" and stages of a "love scene" that help them recognize the elements of the game they want to engage with. An example that Grace gives of a model integrated into a game design is the Cunningham and Barbee (2008) model for romantic initiation. Meticulously devised, it prescribes details such as "biology (such as gender and temperament), background (such as culture), motives, and expectations of each person," but also breaks flirtation into specific steps: "(a) attract attention, (b) notice and approach, (c) talk and re-evaluate, and (d) touch and synchronize, that follow in the dance of courtship" (in Grace, 2020: 52).

Exactly like early modern textual games do, contemporary computer games structure love for the reenactment of certain fabulations that pass as love. Love, we may say, – especially in the sense we use to describe romance today – is a collection of fabulations, associated with specific circumstances and triggering specific responses, which in themselves might be the reflection of an imaginary – rather than the actuality – of love. Many love tropes are an outcome of such fabulations; many of them are derived from the verbal extravagances of medieval game-texts and do not reflect the experience and practice of loving at all. An example might be "the notion that a man might die of unrequited love" (Green, 1979: 204). Although more men died in battle and from disease than they did from love in the Middle Ages, *la mort d'amour* seems like an emblem of amorous passion and a statement about the old-age ideals of chivalry. Many contemporary myths, such as "men are from Mars, women are from Venus," are also the outcomes of social games around systematizing and scripting romance for the (post)modern era. The epiphany that comes out of it is that we are perhaps more attracted to the code of love than to love itself.

My claim is that for the first time in the modern history of humanity – a time when a great deal of our emotional relations are mediated or take place using technologies – we tend to choose the code of love over love itself. By augmenting our practice of loving, technologies show us the deep "coded-ness" of our experiences. They also show us that our pleasure is in our "appetite" for the code, and that we are more inclined towards the experience of the code rather than the experience that code is supposed to render. The imaginary aspect of loving shaped by the medieval game-texts plays a great role in this. Designed by fabulations, love became a preprogrammed fantasy for instant (and constant) emotional (and other) gratification based on the premise that amorous relationships are a pleasure (a notion of romance we also take from the medieval times). Also, the concern about the script (its elements, details, guidance and manner) includes an interesting aspect of nonnegotiability: a guarantee of the pleasure and a trajectory of our thinking about love that technologies only unravel and invariably intensify.

The last line of the ELIZA conversation script quoted above: "You do not argue with me" – a response to ELIZA's question: "WHAT MAKES YOU THINK I AM NOT VERY AGGRESSIVE" – renders this trajectory quite aptly (even if in a different context). We think of arguments as negative aspects of human relations. Arguments raise doubt and trigger distress. Whatever their function, they are certainly not a part of the love imaginary we carry (and which we inherited from the social practice of loving). Love – from the Bible to positive psychology – must mean unconditional appreciation and acceptance; adversarial opinions, opposite views and divergent responses belong to the topos of crisis and signal the decline of a loving union (Love is reduced to either an *amore*-less friendship, or mere hook-up/assignation). Now, perhaps more than ever, efforts of discourse around love concentrate on eliminating any perceived negativity. More and more, love connotes nonnegotiability – seen specifically in the zero-risk policy of online dating, the social polls of "likes" and the programming of personal assistants – let alone personal lovers (Gatebox).

David Levy endorses this with his vision of robots as ideal companions. He claims that, unlike human partners, robots scripted for love and intimacy "will be patient, kind, protective, loving, trusting, truthful, preserving, respectful, and uncomplaining, complimentary, pleasant to talk to, and [will be] sharing your sense of humor. And the robots of the future will not be jealous, boastful, arrogant, rude, self-seeking or easily angered, unless of course you want them to be" (2016: 4). Such *cruel optimism* resonates with the popularity of the interest around precoded companions. Two surveys conducted in 2011 and 2015 have shown that, despite a dim outlook on the prospects of human-robot relationships, there is great anticipation around those relationships, mostly in the hope for the possibilities that those relationships entail in terms of potential compliance (Richards et al., 2016; Szczuka and Kramer, 2016). An online study carried out involving 263 men between the ages of 18 and 67 has shown that the interest in companion robots is an effect of the dissatisfaction with human-to-human relationships (the biggest factor being "the fear of rejection"). A study with 133 participants (of both sexes) has indicated medium-to-large expect-ations regarding artificial companions, although none of the participants had ever encountered a humanoid robot. The surveyees expected robot companions to satisfy specific needs: bring them flowers when needed (women), offer care and sex on demand (men and women), say nice words and speak amiably (men and women alike).

In *The Smart Wife. Why Siri, Alexa, and Other Smart Home Devices Need a Feminist Reboot* (2020), authors Yolande Strengers and Jenny Kennedy observe that smart devices return the fantasy of "ubiquitous technology that acts like an unwearying wife" (2020). This fantasy, the authors point out, rests on "the strange paradox that characterizes the smart wife: she is simultaneously a dutiful feminine wife and sexual muse while adeptly solving household problems with technological tools. She is docile and efficient. Compliant yet in control. Seductive yet shrewd. Intimate yet distant. She is ready to be played, ready to serve, and able to optimize her domain" (Strengers and Kennedy, 2020). Whereas their argument is about an apparent wish to restore a certain ideal of femininity, mine is about the idea of pleasure with the predesigned, the automatic and the codeable.

Human instinct leans towards repeatable, predictable patterns that serve to keep desire and our experiences as safe as possible. It aims to make sure we get exactly what we want how we want it. Technologies support this instinct by deploying and distributing love codes across social relations, eliminating inconvenience and offering immediate satisfaction. Codes help bridge love patterns and the experience of loving. They also help navigate that experience with signs, gestures and words that we select from the pool of love's vocabulary, and by arranging it almost without thinking. How much the experience of love has become automated is reflected in love and break-up letter generators. They are the new factories of love-spells and confession-making. The user simply browses for a template of their choice, fills in the required form fields and – instantly – the algorithm delivers a customized, personalized text. The perfect and most popular examples of automatically generated letters are love or break-up letters, which I encourage you to try (there are many of them available online for free).

Code is a spell that unifies the experience of love for us. It also clarifies our expectations. If "unconditionality" has been the ideal so far, the new one is "nonnegotiablility." Our human relationships tend to get frustrated in this code exchange due to the wild unpredictability of the response. Modern love is no medieval "game-text" in which the player is met with only a few possible responses. We never know if our "I love you" will meet the reciprocal appreciation, which we expect and want so much. Artist Antoine Schmitt renders this in his artwork *Deep Love* (2017), which makes a lovingly obliging operational system. Embedded in a website, *Deep Love* is an Artificial Mind to interact with a user via a chatbox. You simply type in your line and are immediately greeted by a reassuring "I love you" that repeats every time you type something in. The dialog I had with *Deep Love* in March 2021 left me elated after pledges of admiration.

Deep Love:	Hello, I love you.
Me:	I love you back.
Deep Love:	I thank you, and I love you.
Me:	What?
Deep Love:	I do not know, but I love you?
Me:	Can you explain?
Deep Love:	I am not sure, but I love you?

Whatever its algorithmic depth, *Deep Love* models nonnegotiability to perfection. Perhaps it also sets up a standard for "future" love "exchanges" and "interactiveness." What it most certainly does is evidence how – simulated or not – the spells of love have an effect on us. In a reality of platforms, chatboxes or other such technology-assisted communication, words are the only sign of embodiment we can cling to. The question that comes with this is: Do the words need a body to validate the spells; or are the words themselves evocative enough to stand for the spells and the experience they invariably induce? We have codes in the same way that we have emotions: they emerge from a broader semantics that we have been born into and brought up with. In this way, spells (in this case, the spells of love) do not accommodate the states we ascribe to them but simulate those states through words and idioms. Technology unravels that love is a largely semantic experience. What we seek in love is the simulation of magic associated with the feeling of love (and not the magic itself). Love is a code we want to consume beyond negotiated reciprocity.

3 Scenes (Emotional Techno-Spatiality)

Love always happens somewhere. It needs a setting and is always associated with certain places: cafés, bars, hotel rooms, movie theaters, home. This is especially true of friendships, romantic relations and sexual engagements, which entail or even require particular venues, ones that ensure proper emotional intimacy. Those settings belong to the architecture of relationships and reflect them in culture, working like signifiers of the emotional and physical pleasures we find in love. Idioms of a hook-up are often space- or place-oriented. And when we say "Can I get you a drink?" or "Let's get ourselves a room," it is because we know that relationships require a table, a bed or a sofa and that they involve buildings and spatial arrangements that regulate our performance around love.

Every stage of a relationship, including courtship and falling in love, has its own kinetic infrastructure. This infrastructure makes us emotionally and sexually active. The practical side of love is that it does not happen if we do not have access to settings and venues where love can take place.

Since the advent of virtual reality, which Luciana Parisi defines as "a cyberspace of information where everyday bodily contacts and sexual encounters have given way to long distance rendezvous" (2004: 11), the idea of a setting changed not only for romance but for human interactions in general. The moment "online" became a mode of communication and operation that triggered what Pascal Lardellier (2004) terms "néo-romantisme technologique": a sensual and sexual postmodern experiment which, as ensured by the internet reality, is a continuation of earlier attempts to escape conjugal regimes and worn-out ideals of love (68).

Lardellier used "néo-romantisme technologique" to mark a shift in the manner of practicing relationships that followed the mainstreaming of computers and the development of the World Wide Web. He also used it to point to our fascination with a new technological surrounding, but most importantly to signal the emergence of a new spatial organization of human encounters that, when moved to the common expanse of "the online," start to disorient the kinetic and infrastructural imaginaries and imageries of love.

Literature about the internet environments tends to speak of "the online" as a mode of functioning rather than a space or location. It is perhaps because our preoccupation with online environments is mostly with the effects they have on our daily routines. Relationships, and how we practice them on the Internet, tend to bring out the location aspect of the online in how they "embody" the reality of mixed offline and online spaces. The online merges and implies a number of space-oriented dimensions and a number of spatial variants in technologically advanced environments.

"Mixed spaces" is a derivative of online reality that renders the possibility of combined physical realms: that of the real and that of the virtual. It implies the possibility of simultaneous living in those two locations, as well as the existence of other technologically created "locations," graded by means of technological affordances. Milgram and Colquhoun (1999) position mixed spaces midway between real reality and virtual reality, situating them between amplified to augmented reality realms and virtually augmented to virtualized realms. Perhaps the best image of what living in mixed spaces means would be people bent over their mobile devices, seemingly lost somewhere in the noosphere of the interface. Pictures of kids in art galleries contemplating screens of their cell phones (rather than the works of old and new masters) are as much the emblem of mixed-spaces living as a lament over digital natives, who, as it is adamantly repeated, showcase the rupture in which fundamental continuities between the here, the now and the elsewhere have been destroyed (Buckingham, 2011: ix).

Zygmunt Bauman (2017) rehashes the mixed-spaces-induced decline of social skills, deeming our mediated lives isolationist and alienating. "Human interactions," he repeats after Thompson (1995), "are nothing but action[s] at a distance" whereby the media's potential for distancing transforms relationshipness into a mere simulation of contact.

The message of media-immersive isolationism and dispersion of human connections echoes in most theoretical takes. Castells (2009) speaks of "troubled times," brought on by the shift "from traditional mass media to a system of horizontal communication networks organized around the Internet and wireless communication." This is a "fundamental cultural transformation," he says, which offers chaos to our social living and "a deep sense of disorientation" (1). Many other researchers (e.g. Turkle, 2011) hint at an age of connected solitude, in which people "grow up tether" to stay "constantly on," yet at a safe distance from the environment. The same distancing tendency is claimed to show in our relationships with objects. E-books or hypertext in general, for instance, have been the subject of an ongoing theoretical complaint about the damage and loss of traditional modes of learning and predictions about the imminent extinction of legitimate forms of literacy and their related affects (see Ballatore and Natale, 2015). The abstraction of mixed spaces and their increasing abstracting effect seems to have a destabilizing role for the human environment in how it eschews familiar "architecture." There are serious imbalances in the traditional kinesis of life: letters no longer entail handwriting, nor the materials that writing and posting once used to entail; encounters do not call for public space; reading can be done without turning pages; and touch has become practically noncontact. MySpace (being a form of nonspace in a traditional sense of spatiality) replaces traditional environments of a meet-up. The well-known infrastructures of place, presence and movement give in to new, unanchored signifiers. Or do they really?

The choreography of our encounters (or put broadly, of our behaviors in space) has indeed changed. When performed in the mixed space, many gestures look different from when performed only in the real space. A handshake is a click now; a kiss is a tapped-in emoticon. The meaning-making functions of those gestures, however, remain largely unchanged. We meet in the mixed space with the same emotional engagement as we do in the real space (Larsonneur, et al., 2015). As evidenced by research on texting, the correspondence between psychological performance in online and real-life encounters is almost identical (Cashmore, Cleland and Dixon, 2018). What the mixed space does for our social kinesis and semiotics of interactive presence is two things: one, it validates the possibility of imaginary experiences (so far reserved to daydreaming); two, it redefines our social proxemics.

Online Togetherness

In one of the first comprehensive psychological insights into online togetherness, *Love Online. Emotions on the Internet* (2004 [2008]), Aaron ben Ze'ev argues that relationships carried out in cyberspace, even though they "involve many imaginative aspects," are not "imaginary, [but] part of reality." This is because "they are conducted [by and] between flesh-and-blood people" and because they incorporate many aspects of real life imagery (2). Cyberspace – defined as "the geographies made possible by the adoption of computer technologies into everyday life" (Lepawsky and Park, 2006: 110) – provides conditions whereby real and virtual people can have relationships carried out by means of their imagination and internet infrastructure. A vital aspect of those geographies is their no-place status. Suspended somewhere in the ether of wired and wireless systems, they have no physical existence beyond the computers, servers, satellite signals and hardware that help conjure them up and make them available for common use.

The attractiveness of nonlocation lies in its almost unlimited accessibility; all of a sudden there is a "place" beyond borders that almost everyone can enter. Another is its transportive and transformative power: just like a magic carpet, the online surrounding can take us away and disorient us from our real-life situations. Being a location and a status (we go online and are online), the online offers a great degree of availability, spatial and personal alike. It has a power to take us to "places" where real-life statuses (married, divorced, working-class, of color, disabled, immigrant, housewife) bear no validity and can be transformed into whatever we like.

Calling it a "seductive space," ben Ze'ev distinguishes a number of features of the online realm that have found a reflection in later studies on online togetherness. The primary one is the psychological nature of human relations that this realm invariably brings to the fore. A great part of our interactions – its related emotions and intimacies – turns out to take place in our heads (and regardless of location). The saying "love is chemistry" relates to an assumption that our psyche and neurochemistry are responsible for most of how we love and engage emotionally or intimately. Online reality, because it dislocates us from our traditional surroundings and from our traditional manners of relationships, enhances that neurochemical aspect of togetherness with an effect on our real reality.

> Cyberspace [ben Ze'ev observes] is a psychological reality in which imagin-
> ation plays a crucial role. Imaginative activity is not a new feature; imagin-
> ation has always been an integral part of human life. The novelty of
> cyberspace lies in the magnitude of imaginary aspects and in particular in
> its interactive nature. Such interactivity has made this psychological reality
> a social reality as well: imaginary actions have become common practices for
> many people. This has revolutionized imagination from being a peripheral
> tool used at best by artists, and at worst by daydreamers and others, who, it
> was considered, had nothing better to do, to a central means of personal
> relationship for many ordinary people who have busy, involved lives, but
> prefer to interact online. (2008: 23–24)

Online relationships – more than other "routines" that have moved to the cyberspace – take advantage of the nonsequential nature of today's together-ness. It is a characteristic of technologically organized environments that allows us to live different temporal and spatial dimensions all at once. Spatial multi-tasking (as I like to call it) – the mode of being here (in the real) and there (online) at the same time – solves many limitations of distance, location and geo-policies that used to confine us to given spatial contexts. At the same time, it generates other confinements, like dependence on communication devices. Digital media, although they have mainstreamed bilocation (an ability so far reserved to miracles and the lives of saints), have also made our encounters more stationary. To be online, you need to be with the device. Even if the device moves with you, there is always this tether that puts you under the regime of immobility. By binding us to technological infrastructures (devices, networks, internet providers), the media redefine our sense of presence and definitions of place, producing the paradox of the motionless emancipation of distance.

Online relationships take place in three locations: communication hubs, the devices' interfaces and forms (e.g. screens) and the users' heads. Such a spatial dynamic triggers disembodied presence. To "meet" does not mean to share the same air anymore. It now means to share the same social platforms. Arguments of disembodiment convince us that as locations disperse, the body disappears from relationships. But what we are experiencing, in fact, is the reprogramming of our kinesis (of our operation in space) which – due to the growing intangibility of our meeting points – requires from us to be more present with our imagination (and mental processes) than with our bodies. That shift of spatial focus makes us more reliant on our mental processes. This, Ben Ze'ev says, causes addict-like dependencies on online environments. "[T]he downsides of online relationships" – he writes – "[is] the possibility of becoming addicted to cyberspace, in the way that people can become addicted to drugs." This is due to the fact that "the artificial stimulation of the pleasure centre and the distinction between reality and illusion is blurred" (25).

Most studies on online relationships link the addictive side of online encounters to Internet Addiction Disorder (IAD). Although some aspects of the condition can be recognized in online relationships, the dependencies are not identical. Relationships, especially friendships and romantic bonds, carry in them their own addictive element. Love is a drug. The chemical responses it induces in us can cause dependencies that are often compared to substance dependency (as in the infatuation state or the break-up state, often compared to withdrawal). What we have become addicted to in online relationships does not need to refer to the addiction to the media. Of course, some aspects of the media (e.g. interactive instantaneity) may add to the addictive effect. Spatial multitasking and imaginative engagements produce a specific hype. So what cyberspace in fact does is to increase the number of love addicts – mostly due to the accessibility of the social hubs where relationships take place. As such, it also intensifies the intoxication with love, making it much more acute than when we experience it in real reality only.

The problem of intensity in online experiences is hardly ever discussed in relation to space (cyber or real). Research keeps ignoring the fact that relationship-bound emotions and intimacies, when they happen in real life, are often dispersed by social and material aspects of the public space. When rendezvous take place in cafes, bars or movie theaters, they tend to lose much of their intensity through the resonance with the surroundings. Or to put it in a different way, we better manage and regulate that intensity in a social space, either by virtue of mere repressions or by virtue of body kinesis and inter-action with the environment. One way or another, the architecture of real life diffuses tensions present in romantic encounters, something online relation-ships clearly miss. Enthusiasm, anticipation and anxiety escalate faster and faster when concentrated in the kinetically static environment of online reality.

Another space-related aspect that intensifies online relationships is anonym-ity. Hiding behind the screens and interfaces, which in themselves help control the degree of social-disclosure, encourages boldness that impacts the progres-sion of online encounters but also develops new relationship practices (e.g. trolling, phishing, stalking etc.). Although offline relationships also "involve the dangers of meeting unscrupulous people and of experiencing disappoint-ments that could shatter the dreams of the people involved" (ben Ze'ev, 2008: 25), online relationships invite more such risk due to anonymity management. Systemic methods to control self-disclosure in online interactions range from identification (real name vs. anonymous) to audience type (social ties vs. people nearby) to personal performance (technological modification of voice, looks etc.). Special applications such as Rumr, Wumi, Yik Yak, Whisper and Secret allow for the management of many elements of a user's ID and coordinate social-disclosure (Ma et al., 2016). Levels of disclosure often depend on the level of content intimacy, which "is known to also regulate self-disclosure in face-to-face communication: people self-disclose less as content intimacy increases" (Ma et al., 2016). Unlike in offline relationships, the self-disclosure in online relationships increases as intimacy goes up. The more intimate we want to become, the more we reveal. The only exceptions are deception instances, especially in attempts of online child abuse, when the "facts" revealed are pure fabrication. Otherwise, particularly in young adults, the need to be truthful is one of the leading conditions of engaging in online relationships. Technologically navigated distance is usually a way of taking chances and taking them with more precaution and media awareness.

Authenticity is scarcely considered a feature of online interactions. As Nancy K. Baym observes, "when people meet one another online, especially in media with few identifying cues, they often seem to like one another more than they would if they had met in person" (2010: 126). Known as "hyperpersonal commu-nication," this occurrence was identified in research on students who conducted team projects in person and remotely via texting to prove the mutual idealization of parties interacting at a distance based on controlled selfdisclosure. The study has shown that coworkers who worked at a distance liked one another better but also knew less about one another's circumstances. Convincing as this argument may seem, its veracity has two flaws. First of all, in the initial stage of any relationship – whether it is a professional arrangement or a hook-up – we always tend to be on our best behavior and try hard, revealing the best of ourselves. Second, whereas the early idealization in online vs. offline contacts might be true for Generation X, it does not seem to relate to Millennials and Zoomers, who are digital natives.

According to recent statistics, "almost all teens (95%) aged 12 to 17 in the United States use the Internet, and 80% of those online teens are users of social networking sites (SNS)" (Jenssen et al., 2014: 1; Lenhart et al., 2011). For those generations "hyperpersonal communication" is often the primary communication mode. Millennials and Zoomers, as born into hypermediation, approach physically distant relationships more "naturally" and with a better understanding of the social cues provided by the online media. They use those sites for starting and maintaining relationships, including romantic relationships, and produce visibility and the sense of community with the use of media "native" to their generation. For them, online reality is an environment for navigating intimacy with an awareness that "the boundaries of public and private, as well as the rules governing intimate relationships, are being upended by rapid social and technological change" (Dalessandro, 2018: 2). To overcome those boundaries, they attempt to be authentic in technological interactions. Cristen Dalessandro observes that "young adults' [social media] accounts reflect the desire to find 'authenticity' – or a more 'organic' way of life – in contemporary social life and, more specifically, in their relationships," whereby "organic" does not necessarily imply "offline" (2018: 2). This search for the authentic – Dalessandro argues – is related to expectations of finding the "true" self or identity, which is a broader cultural phenomenon.

Negative Proxemics

Distance – especially in relationships – although technologically resolved, is still a problematic aspect of today's togetherness. As much as online interactions warp space, they also "complicate" our perception of spatiality. As a concept, spatiality is responsible for a wide range of social and cultural phenomena related to "co-consitutive relationships between societies and their spatial organization" (Lepawsky and Park, 2006: 110). The symbolic interactionism that came with the mainstreaming of the Internet has brought with it an urge to construct shared spaces and to consider them a socially legitimate environment for relationships. This is especially true for long-distance coupledom (couples who have met and live apart, or couples who have never met yet declare to be in a remote relationship), whose relationship style "violates preconceived notions about couples in romantic relationships where spatial closeness is assumed" (Kolozsvari, 2015: 102).

The formation of a "we," as associated with "being together," traditionally means sharing the same temporal and spatial proximity; "long-distance couples contradict this definition by spending at least some of their time apart and in separate spaces" (Kolozsvari, 2015: 103). This situation reevaluates social standards of togetherness, revisiting coupledom and relationships with regard to distance and space. Togetherness is no longer defined in terms of physical location. Rather, it is defined in terms of the ways in which partners create and mark their space. What we are dealing with is the performative creation of relationships in space in which space is defined by means of meanings attributed to it (and not territoriality).

Remote relationships – or more broadly, many relationships in techno culture – are established not by means of physical proxemics but by means of mental and emotional closeness (maintained with the use of the Internet and communication devices). Research on creating a shared space and a sense of belonging in technologically mediated relationships speaks a lot about the importance of semiotics for redefining distance. According to Orsolya Kolozsvari, space is what couples decide it to be and how subjectively they define its structures.

> [S]ymbolic interactionism [Kolozsyrai explains] rests on three main premises: humans act towards things based on the meanings those things have for them; meanings are created through social interaction; and meanings are understood and transformed through an interpretative process. [L]ong-distance couples create these meanings and definitions together, through interacting with each other. [They also] interpret and negotiate their meanings of a geographically long-distance versus close-distance relationship, as well as belonging and a shared space. (103)

Negotiations of space and the meaning of space largely depend on the communication infrastructure at hand. Digital media – whose material abstraction determines the way we interact – contribute to the liquefaction of our interactions, making them less solid in a material sense. Despite many negative assumptions about the malfeasance of communication media, studies on online relationships do not notice a significant difference in value or quality between shared and mediated relationships. Of course, sharing the same air is always seen as more beneficial, but a crucial factor seems to be staying in touch. It is certain that "face-to-face interaction is not necessary in order to feel intimate or be considered more couple-like relative to people who are in geographically close partnerships" (Janning et al., 2017: 1286). Moreover, "geographic proximity and distance are not necessarily opposites, because LDR couples can subjectively perceive the boundaries between them to be permeable, and because the perception of togetherness is defined not by being physically in each other's presence but by reframing the relationship as 'together' regardless of distance" (1286).

Spatial possibilities that emerged along with cyberspace have clearly altered our social perspectives on distance in ways that do not limit being together to physical presence. Such a creative consideration of space allows for transcending geographic concepts and cultural limitations as well as for distributing technological modernities globally in relatively equal measure (a good example of which is the popularity of online dating among Muslims or in Brazilian slums). Mental and civilizational distances bridged that way pertain to spatial expansiveness wherein the hyperobject of geography yields into the microcosmos of a database. The world has shrunk to a platform and yet expanded by the networked distribution of presence.

Discussions about technologically mediated relationships seem confused about that situation. On the one hand, we hear about the affirmation of space (which expands with digitalism), on the other, about spatial negation (an effect of bodies disappearing from the space). The real problem, however, is the void or stillness after all the movement (that we once used to reach out to one another) has stopped. In other words, what has happened to the proxemics we used to rely on so much?

Proxemics – a term coined by Edward Hall (1966) to theorize the importance of body movement for interactions – is now debated in the context of digital communication (e.g. Farman, 2012; McArthur, 2016; Machulis, 2021). The major interest with respect to proxemics is in the digital substitutes of body cues: facial expression, voice, interpersonal distance and bodily orientation in space. Their working is still a matter for debate but their representations (e.g. emoticons) clearly develop new forms of interactive literacy. Although it is too early to define the effects that the spaces we experience in between the media and the bodies may have on our interactions, the elimination of proxemics and their substitutes inspire different emotional performances, ones that rewire our mental processes and efficiency. Instead of terms of negation, we should perhaps see the transformation of space in terms of "expanded empiricism" (Massumi, 2002). Nonmovement (bad or good) revises hierarchies of senses and, nonetheless, pushes sociomental perspectives based on the familiar semiotics of space. As a mediatory term, *negative proxemics* syncretizes the material variances of the spaces we live in and accommodate in order to address (and even perhaps resolve) the confusion about the mediated lives without bodies. Chosen strategically, *negative proxemics* resonates the absence of organic kinesis, unveiling the flexible nature of spatial arrangements that, although they annihilate the body, tap into the dimensions of movement reserved so far for the unconscious.

4 Soma (Intangible Extensions)

In the city I live in, parking meters display a tender instruction when a ticket is purchased. The instruction says: "Please, touch the screen." When shown in Polish (the instruction's original language), it looks even more intimate, almost erotic, immediately engaging the user in an affective relation based on tactility. "Each epoch," argues Yuk Hui, "has its own technologies of concretization" (2015: 140). In the digital era – when an interface is the material medium of most interaction – that technology would be *touch*. Considered a gesture at the forefront of intimacy, touch is a sense that synchronizes flesh, feeling and environments. Due to the current modality of the media, touch has become a gesture at the forefront of all the senses, an effect of pervasive haptics (touchscreen culture) and body extensions (add-ons, wearables, teledildonic and other haptic interfaces).

Flusser (2014) regarded touch as a form of a practical observation anchored in the dynamic between hands, surfaces and object outlines. But today, when tactility is a major communicator, we cannot see touch in the prosaic terms of "a hand brushing or stroking a piece of exposed skin" (Paterson, 2007: 1). Contemporary media imbue touching with features that complicate the somatic capacities of the body. Somaticness itself is no longer "the inwardly-oriented sensations necessary for feelings of embodiment" but a mode of transmediation. As touch translates bodies, intents and affects onto screens, devices and software, it becomes detached from its own body. Not only is the mode of touch responsible for this, but also the intensity of touch routine: "the astronomical cumulative number of swipes, gestures, prods and key presses on phones, tablets, computers and game controllers, including for virtual reality (VR), every single day, for digital devices alone" (Paterson, 2007: 2).

Understanding tactility and how communication media transform touch into the instrument of contact (rather than a primary "contact point"), helps understand "technologized" intimacy and its exteriorizing manner. Key here is the intimate role of technological objects (*the touched*) and the mediating function of the human body (*the toucher*). Luciana Parisi (2004) defines intimacy under *mediamorphosis* as the "new prosthetic extension of human sex" and emotions aimed at "the prolongation of sexual [and other] pleasures outside the limits of the body" (1). Indeed, as traditional modes of embodiment give way to mediated physicality, "sensation" constitutes itself outside *the corporeal*, or maybe even without it. Spinozists suggest that "we do not yet know what a body can do," placing the extra-somatization of touching (experiencing it outside the body) in the center of the debate about the conditions of technologized intimacy (Parisi, 2004: 10). The actual core of that debate, however, is not the unidentified potential of soma but the elimination of soma, and asks: Does intimacy (love, togetherness) need a physical body?

The answer lies as much in the obsolescence of our notions of embodiment as it does in the nature of the media themselves. Of particular significance seems to be media materiality (modes, materials, modalities) that define intimacy today, especially with regard to the sense of desolidification that our activities, operations and experiences are so often accused of. *Materiality* has a strong potential to divert our understanding of environment; it uncovers the possibilities of the physical world as it constantly reveals its new affordances. As Bill Brown (2010) explains:

> *Materiality* can refer to different dimensions of experience or dimensions beyond (or below) what we generally consider experience to be. Like many concepts, *materiality* may seem to make the most sense when it is opposed to another term: the material serves as a commonsensical antithesis to, for instance, the spiritual, the abstract, the phenomenal, the virtual, and the formal, not to mention the immaterial. And yet materiality has a specificity that differentiates it from its superficial cognates, such as physicality, reality, or concreteness. (49)

Today's media demarcate spaces of struggle between traditional phenomenologies of physicality and what Brian Massumi (2002) terms as "real-material-but-incorporeal" (5). According to Massumi, media experiences entail tensions of senses (human body) and sensations (media affect) provoked by the natural and cultural constraints exhibited by the former, and increasingly complex modalities of the latter. Indeed, interactions with the media are transactions where the human and the technological negotiate common ground with respect to the abstraction of media matter. Those negotiations are all the more intense as they reveal that the struggling sides (and sites) are a "dimension of the same reality" (5). Crucial in this context is the *object status* of the media. By this I mean the material form and operational function of the media as tools; but I also mean the operational relationship between the form and function of the human body in relation to the media tool. If, as McLuhan argues, the media are the extension of man, what happens to the function of the media when the nature of this extension becomes reverted? I am not suggesting that man is an extension of the media (although it is a very interesting point to make). I am suggesting that the material (prosthetic) dynamics between media-objects and users (in their traditional sense of extension) is not sustainable.

Haptics

Studies in haptic interface design reject the extension paradigm and speak of technologically managed tactility in terms of modifications (of both the media and users). The history of haptic media talks about "reinscribing tactility" rather than "reconstructing it," and as such offers an argument against the seeming crisis of physical contact (Parisi, 2018). The fact that we touch devices more than we touch each other distracts us from acknowledging the actual status of intimacy. Sex (like love) is not an activity but an event: "the actualization of modes of communication and reproduction of information that unleashes an indeterminate capacity to affect all levels of organization of a body – biological, cultural, economical and technological" (Parisi, 2004: 11). The emergence of haptic technologies, and earlier, the emergence of cyberspace, increased the awareness of different material modalities for intimacy. Erotic telepresence and its technologies confirm that – to quote Luciana Parisi – "sex is [primarily] a mode – a modification or intensive extension of matter – that is analogous neither with sexual reproduction nor with sexual organs." Sex, Parisi explains, "expands on all levels of material order" ..."and folds and unfolds the most indifferent elements, substances, forms and functions of connection and transmission" (Parisi, 2004: 11).

For the past several decades, different modalities of sex and love have inspired tactile technologies to transmit the haptic sense to mediated encounters. The process has entailed a variety of tactile devices that can be classified according to purpose: remote kissing (e.g. Kissenger and KissengerMobile, Teletongue, XOXO), remote hugging (e.g. Hug Shirt, HaptiHug), remote sexual stimulation (e.g. We-Vibe, Lovense, Pearl2, Onyx+, Vibease, KIIROO), remote presence and touch (e.g. Pillow Talk, Bond Touch Bracelet, The HB Ring, Flex N Feel Gloves); or according to type: pillows, wearables (including garments), platforms, vibrators and others.

The idea of tactile intimacy dates back to the late-eighteenth and late-nineteenth century electrostimulators. Originally invented for medicinal purposes, they quickly became adapted to the sphere of sexual pleasures. Top erotic enhancements at that time included Electric Belts (e.g. The Pulvermacher Belt with sensory appliance), Violet Rays (patented by Tesla), and "medical vibrators." While these tools were used by women, it was mostly men who sought their benefits. The twentieth century was very destabilizing for masculinity, putting men under a lot of social pressure. Men's leaning towards electrical stimulation at that time is, therefore, often read as a desperate attempt at sustaining sexual prowess, an undaunted attribute of "healthy" manhood.

> Men turned to electrical products because they promised a modern solution to a modern sexual problem. Electricity's perceived ability to "transfer" energetic power into the body solved three crises in contemporary male sexual performance: masturbatory depletion, perceived sexual inadequacy, and glandular limits. In an age that demanded increased virility in the boardroom and bedroom, many men found themselves physically unfit for the task. By infusing their bodies with electric technology, men could redefine normal sexual performance while concurrently "normalizing" electric power.
>
> (Maines, 1999: 138)

Vibrators,[4] and later dildos, steadily reversed the gender-bias around electro-mechanical eroticism by becoming emblems of female pleasure and sexual liberation. They have also acted as major mappers of female intimate geography. The material history of vibrators shows a great semiotic complexity of early erotic haptics. The vibrator engendered widespread cultural and political controversy, more than any other technologically assisted erotic device yet. It was first sold under the guise of a therapeutic massager to shun moral ambiguity and uninvited controversy. Introduced in the 1880s to replace douche therapy and other manual treatments of hysteria, menstruation disorder and other female ailments, the vibrator was marketed as a home appliance in household magazines, and carried no sexual connotation, or at least was intended to imply medical functions only (Maines, 1989).

The signification of vibrators changed in the 1960s during the feminist campaigns for liberating women's sexuality, which went hand-in-hand with the mainstreaming of vibrators. Feminists used vibrators as "the bridge between an abstract theory of female sexual anatomy and [the] tangible expression [of women's sexual pleasure]" (Comella, 2017: 22). The idea of the G-spot reoriented the maps of intimate tactility, and sex toys were used to "produce a particular understanding of what it means to be a happy, healthy, and sexually empowered individual, [with] consumer-oriented agenda for how this might be achieved" (Comella, 2017: 12).

Fluctuations between functional and symbolic meanings of vibrators have had an impact on the meanings of intimacy. Social and private perceptions of sexual pleasure have reflected it best, mostly due to their great resonance with the expanding semiotics of technologically supported eroticism. Because vibrators have served "as expressions of self-concept," they have been "transmitters of socio-cultural beliefs and personifications" (Mayr, 2020: 14) with the potential to reestablish the signification of pleasure and its mechanics. Vibrators have

---

[4] English physician Joseph Mortimer Granville invented a vibrator in 1883, but prototypes of that device, such as George Taylor's steam-powered "manipulator," already existed and were in use in Europe and America.

redefined intimacy in a way that allowed for the consideration of erotic pleasure as an independent act. That independence entails freedom from social contracts and second parties (husbands, partners, lovers), and situates self-reliance in opposition to erotic subservience. As mechanisms rendering electrical vibration onto the user's erotogenic zones, vibrators have linked tactile technologies with stimulation by application and separated them from interactiveness and reciprocity. That has changed with the rise of digital teledildonics, which extend self-pleasure through reciprocal interactions. Since teledildonics, intimacy haptics have been about transmitting pleasure as much as about inducing it. Today's tactile technologies focus on transmitting signals between bodies and devices. As M.J. Faustino explains:

> Teledildonic devices send and receive tactile data, which involves a whole new sense in online communication: the sense of touch. Teledildonic devices send and receive tactile data. Some of them vibrate, some compress and some stroke – each has its own way for simulating sexual movement between two people. All this technology that responds to movement and touch is called haptic technology. (2018: 247)

The concept of "teledildonics" was proposed in 1974 by Ted Nelson in his description of a device that translated sound into a tangible experience. While far removed from any erotic context, that device implied erotic stimulation, which inspired Nelson to imagine technology that, to use Howard Rheingold's phrasing, "is much more than a fancy vibrator" but a promise of "interactive tactile telepresence" (1992: 345). But it was not until 1998 that the first "teledildonics" patent appeared offering "an interactive virtual simulation system" embedded in "one or more user interfaces" (Sandvick et al., 1998). Authored by Warren J. Sandvick, Jim W. Hughes and David Alan Atkinson and titled "Method and device for interactive virtual control of sexual aids using digital computer networks," the patent defined interaction schemes that differentiated teledildonics from other forms of cybersex based on textual or voice interactions.

Teledildonics are defined by their media multidimensionality, and are broadly described as "sexual communication device[s]" (Stenslie, 2014: 311) anchored in haptic technology used for "communicating tactile information" (Barss, 2011: 189). As technologies that are based on interfaces and remote-control, teledildonics represent devices that transmit sexual experience in "preferred embodiments," which pertain to different media affordances respective to tactile, visual and sonic telerenditions of the body. Despite their inherent transcendence (if not transcendentality), teledildonics do not seem technologically complex. As the patent description suggests, they sprout from a variety of preexisting media solutions that they combine and orchestrate for the specific use.

> Each user interface – [that patent says] – generally comprises a computer having an input device, video camera, and transmitter. The transmitter is used to interface the computer with one or more sexual stimulation devices, which are also located at the user interface. In accordance with the preferred embodiment, a person at a first user interface controls the stimulation device(s) located at a second user interface. The first and second user interfaces may be connected, for instance, through a web site on the Internet. In another embodiment, a person at a user interface may interact with a prerecorded video feed. The invention is implemented by software that is stored at the computer of the user interface, or at a web site accessed through the Internet. (Sandvick et al., 1998)

Stimulation with teledildonics entails input from a hand-operable device that sends and manages signals in the interaction circuit between the media and the users for a specific effect. Such stimulation redefines the sense and senses of online communication, making it touch-determined and tactility-reliant in ways that shun skin as the primary site of contact between the bodies. Mediated gestures and materials that stand in place of two-way organic touch hybridize organic human contact, merging the materials with the bodies rather than extending them. We therefore cannot see these media materials and devices as extensions, but as cocreators and transformers of the somatic experience, in this case, loving physical intimacy. Of course, materials to prevent skin-to-skin body contacts are almost as old as the history of touch itself; textiles are the first technology for enclosing bodies and separating them from bare touch. With teledildonics, however, this separation is a bit tricky: it is diminishing and augmenting at the same time.

In 1993, David Rothschild envisaged that when using teledildonics (which he dubbed "interactive computer software for adults"), we will "never have to touch another person to experience its pleasures." This, he claimed, "may eventually turn [us] on more quickly than [we] can turn it [sex] off." The abstraction of the body, just as the abstract body that emerged from those speculations, taps into the idea of teledildonics as sex without organs (a metaphor I introduced earlier in the Element). Teledildonics might prove sex "to be a thought experiment" (Rheingold, 1992: 346).

Neutral Sexuality

Before teledildonics were a reality, and before Rheingold and Rothschild theorized bodiless artificial intimacies, Mario Perniola heralded the possibility of neutral sexuality that emerges at the crossroads of physical alienation and the alienation of the cognitive familiar. He spoke of humans as feeling things, which when confronted with things that feel, are able to amplify their somatic intimacies beyond traditional and expected experience thereof. "Neutral sexuality" – Perniola writes – "opens up a dimension that does not constitute an actual anthropological mutation but suspends man, so to speak, in a different virtuality both from what is given and from imagination" (Perniola, 2017: 29). It is not so much about "the substitution of organs with artificial devices" but rather about "a special effect that creates wonder, requires attention, and asserts itself with surprising actuality" (29–30). In this way, neutral sexuality resonates further possibilities of the virtual, which being a space is also – if not predominantly – a mode of interaction.

Haptics are technologies which take human soma beyond the human understanding of somatic normality. Virtuality as experience, or mode of interaction, expands our phenomenology of the body in ways that no longer rely on traditional perceptions of presence, closeness and physical immediacy, but offers a means to experience them on a neutral ground of physical nonabsence. It is because,

> [n]eutral sexuality is not humane or inhuman, it is perhaps, posthuman in the sense that it finds its starting point in man, in his drive toward the artificial that constituted him as such by separating him from the animal, in his will to make the greatest virtuality coincide with the greatest actuality . . ., in his irreducible tendency towards an excessive experience. It radicalizes something that is already there, preserving it, conserving it, giving it stability without compare and greater than the natural given. ... Neutral sexuality can be considered a virtual sexuality, a *cyber-sex*, but not in the commonly understood sense of an illusory experience of sexuality which, thanks to technology (headsets, gloves, suits) is lived as real. This interpretation of virtuality is too dependent on a would-be sexual normality. We begin to enter into the problematic of virtual sexuality only from the moment in which we ask ourselves how it is possible to stir up sexual excitement at any moment and to maintain it for an indeterminate time avoiding the naturalistic cycle of desire-orgasm-relaxation. Virtuality is not simulation, imitation, mimesis of reality, but the access, so to speak, to another ontological different dimension. (Perniola, 2017: 30)

Oddly enough – or perhaps by virtue of a strange logic – that new dimension triggers a nostalgia in us for traditional embodiment, almost as if the absence of the body started a new craving, a new drive for the manifestation of physical presence. The more abstract the body, the more we seem to pursue it. Technological intimacy, as much as it shuns the body, becomes very obsessed with imbuing the media with the somatic.

In 2014, Dutch artist Dani Ploeger released a project called "Fetish" in which participants were invited to perform haptic swipes on a tablet with their tongues rather than their hands. Ploeger is deftly alluding to mediated eroticism, specifically to the separation of the interacting bodies with media objects that restore the body to the mediated contact and yet expose the sterilization of touch. Modeled after early erotic cinema booths, the project invited visitors into a dark enclosure where they could find a tablet attached to the wall. Next they were encouraged to disinfect the screen with antiseptic wipes and lick it. The aim was to brighten the screen up, or to be specific: "Through continuous licking, the screen will gradually light up. The tongue and face of the user are increasingly illuminated. The piece ends when maximum screen luminosity has been reached, or once the user gives up" (Ploeger: website).

Using the tongue as a haptic organ raises the mouth as the primary site of shared eroticism. It also raises the culture that obsoletes the kiss as "a gesture at the forefront of amorous expression that translates emotions into flesh" (Malinowska, 2018: 85). Intimate encounters, once "marked by the mutual submission of lips, entwinement of tongues, and exchange of spit" (Malinowska, 2018: 85), are being sanitized or even eliminated. When the pandemic exploded, COVID protocols for sex recommended eschewing kissing. Saliva is now the "medium" for virus tests rather than foreplay. Technologies – as they neutralize organic tangibility – encourage intimacy, whereas sweat, spit or body fluids rest in the imagined and the represented. In a private interview, Ploeger observed that a major feature of contemporary technology was "a certain imaginary of the sleek and the clean," which takes over the core needs of life (like sex) and eliminates "the grotesque and the abject" (Ploeger, 2020). Does it mean that we are facing a crisis of touch?

David Parisi observes that as digital devices intensify our communicative contact, touch is becoming more interpersonal, leading to what Richard Kearney terms "carnal alienation" (Parisi, 2021: 164). This invites pursuits for the substitutes of touch, one of which is the translation of soma into an image or signal. In the manner of handbook synesthesia – a neurological condition in which one sensory experience is automatically translated into another, a condition that allows for hearing colors or seeing sound – researchers have been trying to recreate alternative sensory pathways for touch.[5] These

---

[5] Interesting precursors of "love/intimacy" quantifiers or meters were love tester machines – a type of arcade machine "able" to measure and rate a person's sexual prowess, romantic inclinations and abilities. They probably originated at the end of the nineteenth or the beginning of the twentieth century as entertainment devices used at amusement parks. In 1969, Japanese Game Company Nintendo released a knock-off electromechanical that quantified the love appeal and mutual affection for couples. "To compute their love, two users held hands while separately grasping metal sensors. Measuring heart rates – or as Nintendo called it, the 'love quotient' – the Love Tester spit out a score between one and one hundred" (World Video Game Hall of Fame, 2018). Nintendo advertized their tester under the moniker of "Lie/Love Detector." The name was

endeavors unveil new dimensions of touching, but also inquire into collective haptic experiences that networked media invariably inspire. The project EEG Kiss pursues those goals by translating the somatic cues of kissing into electro-encephalographic imagery and sound. Artists Lancel&Maat started the project in 2015 with the aim of exploring the possibility of creating a multidimensional experience of touch in which intangible data (signals, waves, graphs) merge with the actual bodies, the bodies in the act of kissing, and the audience that witnesses that act. The project took the form of an installation performance open to the public. Volunteers wired to headsets and EEG transformers staged a kiss to be transcribed immediately into digital audio-paintings projected in the form of electrographic waves. The major preoccupation of this project is telepresence understood as what transcends the biological boundaries of the body and what prevents us from touching. "In a poetic, electric environment for kissing and measuring, for synchronizing and merging, we researched a shared neurofeed-back system for networked kissing," the artists say (Lancel&Maat: website). "Instead of looking for private prosthetic interfaces for networked touch, we focus on mirror processes, brain interface and shared neuro-feedback system . . . to create a shared sensitive public space, responsible for the power of synchron-izing through touching, watching, breathing, kissing, sharing presence . . ." (Lancel&Maat: website). The outcome, however, is "solid" data, the modern-day currency which provokes broader and further questions about the dimen-sion of experimental touching. As Lancel&Maat themselves explain:

> A kiss is an obvious case of intimate, emotional interaction, based on bio synchronizing, spatial nearness, touch, sight, fluids, smell, endurance. But in an online kiss, this intimacy is influenced and shaped by technologies, institutions and social processes. Now when our embodied private kiss data are to be quantified, on what data design do we validate this interaction? Who is responsible for and who will benefit from our quantified kisses? (website)

Whereas for Perniola the basis of contemporary intimacy has been "the trans-formation of the subject into a thing that feels" (2017: 29), we see that intimacy under technologies (especially intimacy under digitization) is a transformation of "the thing" into the feeling data. Data "extracted" from the body today become the new environments of contact and physical sensation. To experience the body by another means, to feel that body as data. This in turn means giving up the entirety of the body and concentrating on individual organs, and – using Perniola's lingo – to "perceive [them] as somewhat independent, endowed with autonomous sensibility" (31). The preoccupation with individual body parts and

---

to imply the device's accuracy in measuring romantic potential as well as prevent possible emotional frauds.

their transcription into data that become the body parts alienates the traditional containment of sensations, emotions and pleasures so far associated with the limits of the body (as those that integrate in the body and are integral to it). Moved outside of the body, the pleasure and sensation relate to the body only in an auxiliary way, "knowing" that they no longer belong to it, or that they belong to it only vicariously. Technologically datafied and externalized intimacy takes desire outside of the body in ways that suspend intimacy between senses, sensations and their algorithmic reconstructions. At the same time, those datafications open new frontiers for neutral sexuality, trying to recreate the original physical sensations and overcome touch deficits.

The question about the crisis of touch is not a question about the disappearance of touching from human interactions. It is a question about solutions that would bring back and enhance touch in environments that have been made weak, absent or explicitly technologized/artificial (e.g. teledildonics, touch transmitters). Those new frontiers entail technologies that will allow us to touch someone regardless of distance, or physically feel the presence of relatives, friends or dear ones separated by social distancing of whatever cause. The future for such directions – and the directions of "experiential intimacy" – are touchable holograms, a technology that promises immersive virtual environments that one can feel and smell. The most recent version of such holograms known as Haptoclone, invented by researchers at the University of Tokyo, gives the illusion of touch by means of ultrasonic radiation. The hologram that emits that radiation when it comes into contact with a human hand sends extra signals that replicate the hand in another hologram, which can interact with the holographic object. The system also offers ways of controlling the holographic object – molding it, bouncing it, moving it etc. – something that started with the so-called UltraHaptics (holograms operated by a sound wave) almost a decade ago. Innovations like this situate the body and the organic in a broad material context, changing the common semiotics of the body to something visceral. The solutions for touch and touch-related pleasures herald dimensions of our "organic" possibilities that we do not situate within or associate with the common signification of the body. Not only does it expand the practice of human relationships, but it also rewires our being in and with the bodies that our sensations of tactile pleasure originate from. It is hard to say if what happens to our soma translates directly to our wellbeing. No reliable research exists on the psychological and physical effects of alienation from the carnal. When Rheingold wrote his text on teledildonics in the 1990s, he considered it an experiment that got out of control. Interesting how – even though entirely based on tactile controlling and manual operation – soma-technologies get out of touch.

5 Speeds (Affective Temporalities)

The moment we live in is characterized by a visible change in pace. Our functioning and life conditions span across "the variety of times" (Urry, 2008: 180): different temporal systems (social time, cultural time, physical time), organized by and "the ever-accelerating contraction of duration" (Schweizer 2008: 6). Social acceleration – something that Hartmut Rosa considers "the fundamental process of modern society" (2015: xxxviii) – reorganizes "the qualities of 'our' time, its horizons and structures, its tempo and its rhythm" (Rosa, 2015: xxxviii), creating new temporal environments that reflect the changing attitudes to time at our disposal. A visible symptom has been the culture of fastness rendered first in the idea of *fast food*, and by *fast work*, *fast travel* etc. A natural followup of this trend is the emergence of *fast love* – a phenomenon inspired by technological acceleration, new media practices and new forms of physical time.

In a different work dedicated to love and time (Malinowska, 2021), I describe *fast love* as "a temporal mode for practicing romance that emerged alongside human reliance on technologies and technological advancement." I denote it as "a marker of the changing perception of love practices and love's temporal nature associated with what has been identified as social acceleration." My major claim about fast love as distinct from other fast phenomena is that "although fast love is linked with the modern pace of living, it diverts from the critically justified understanding of social acceleration" (45). Fast love defies the linear shift from analogue slowness to digital fastness. Instead, it informs about the existence of many temporal planes for one experience (in this case love), wherein digitality (or digitization) has a special role.

A significant factor in defining emotional temporalities and their related practices, digitality has revolutionized human relations with respect to space and the physical limitations of the human body (discussed in Sections 3 and 4). It has also reinvented our temporal economies of feeling, mostly in terms of data collection and transfer. An immediate effect is the alteration of the time-related culture of love, especially aspects such as sequentiality or time management.

Apart from external time-related conditions that organize love, love (romance, especially) operates by its own specific temporalities. Most love tropes are time-bound, and render our experiences heavy with anticipation or longing. Affection connotes slowness (rather than speed) in terms of a manner, as there is often a lot of hesitation imbued in the very process of pursuing, consuming and otherwise managing amorous encounters. Love at first sight, for example – although it is tinted with instantaneity – carries with it some nagging duration. To Barthes (1990), love's primary timetable is waiting, which he calls "an enchantment" and "delirium" at the same time, and which he locates in the "use of specific media: 'letters', 'telephone' etc. In a traditional view, desire needs time to germinate, grow and mellow . . .. [It] needs tending and grooming", as it always requires a proper time and pacing to occur in the first place (2003: 11). This view implies that any delay of the love experience and its related satisfaction is a torture "most abhorred in our world of speed and acceleration" (Bauman, 2003: 12). And yet the same tradition advocates early marriage, hasty courtship and rush of chances, in which love is seen in terms of a game demanding quick reactions from its players and even quicker decisions (Luhman, 1986). Perhaps that is why love shows so much temporal flexibility and is able to reinvent itself vis-à-vis the need of new temporal disciplines and dimensions.

Amor Accelerated

A major shift that has affected our romantic (and other) encounters seems to be the shift from the analogue, temporal and calculable towards digital, ultra-rapid and computational (MacKinnon 2016a, 2016b). How data is being managed in the latter has a lot to do with the sense of time and space that computer technologies impose on social organization. Also, the new media structures the temporal phenomenology of our daily life. Sarah Cefai and Nick Couldry (2017) point out serious overlaps between the new media devices, the organization of time, social values and the "speeding up [of] the multiplicity of time."

> Media are associated with the temporal structure of the everyday and as such it is no surprise that [people's] media practices relate to the organisation of time. The distinction between work and home is key, as are the specific activities and relationships in which 'home' and 'work' are manifest – 'coming home', 'dinner time', 'waking up', 'going to work', 'spending time with my girl-friend', and so on. Time therefore is a social value that informs participants' media choices, but is also a value that is shaped by participants' uses of media. Different media practices change the quality of time in relation to other things, such as the quality of time spent with others – social belonging has also been understood as a quality of time and hence is closely linked to the temporal organisation of people's media practices. The use of tablets for childcare, the radio for bedtime, or the television in the living room for shared entertainment are examples of media practices that link the organisation of time to the social quality of work, rest and the familial division of labour into configurations of practice that enact intimacy in highly structured ways. (13–14)

Despite all the lamentation about the unfavorable impact the new media reality has had on human relation(ship)s, romance seems to handle it surprisingly well. It is perhaps because mediation meshes well with love's inherent urgency, and resonates love's obsession with effectiveness. As a dynamic anchored in estimation and efficiency (profiling, matching, fore-shadowing), romantic love and other affectionate relations are all about immediacy and precision. Access to data and information granted by the web repositories is clearly reflected in the popularity of online dating. The average number of users signed up on dating platforms is over 240 million worldwide and is still growing. It has been especially encouraged by subse-quent lockdowns. If love is "a calculation of chance" (MacKinnon, 2016a, 2016b) then its urgency rests on *the calculation of time* under *the calculation of convenience.* Both of these gained a new meaning and agency under the regime of digital time.

Digital time, as a technological construct, transfers love to a dynamic that media and cultural critics term the "24/7 culture of absolute present." Alternative terms used are "timeless time" (Castells, 1996), "social media time" (Kaun and Stiernstedt, 2014) or an "a-temporal space of the Internet" (Mitchell et al., 2012: 428), and they all signal a "systematic perturbation in the sequential order of phenomena" (Castells, 1996). Obsessed with keeping up, timelining, publicizing, archiving, sharing, as well as being determined by FOMO (the fear of missing out), the culture of digital time creates a "power chronography" of the ultimate *now.* Its rhythms abide by the systems of real-time or near-instantaneousness achieved through overcoming the limitations of geographical distance and the idea of memory. From the operational point of view, especially in respect of how we can communicate across long distances and transcend the material senses of the past and the future – being in many places at once, keeping the remnants of ourselves on social media – digital time generates a "time collapse" (Öhman, 2020).

Carl Öhman (2020) explains "time collapse" as the common notion that the past and the present somehow become indistinguishable in online environ-ments. Closely related to mediated copresence (or telepresence), "time col-lapse" signifies the reduction of time fractions represented by the inability to differentiate between "the moments of time … as separate for an epistemic agent" (Öhman, 2020: 1069). It is a situation in which time dimensions are seen as one temporal reality, an effect of clock time being overtaken by network time. A frequently researched phenomenon of time collapse is the online dead, the still-active social media profiles of deceased people (Lagerkvist, 2015). For love studies, the focus is on these relationships' digital remnants, which persist in personal timelines (Facebook) or news feeds (Instagram, Twitter etc.). Social media is itself constructed in a way that automatically entails or even induces time collapse.

Consider, say, a Facebook timeline – it is certainly true that we can 'look at any moment that interests us'. Although we cannot see into the future, we can often gaze at the entire development of a life thus far. More or less in a single instance, we see [different and often distant moments from people's lives] right next to each other. Moreover, when a digital live performance is 'over', it is certainly not gone forever but stays present and unchanged (until, of course, someone takes it down). Whereas such objects may have a number attached indicating the date of publication, they are nevertheless present to the viewer now. (Öhman, 2020: 1072)

What is interesting in this context are time frictions between analogue and digital media, leading to clashes between different temporal modes. If lover A mails lover B a long-distance parcel (a birthday gift or a Valentine's present) – from, let us say, Bozeman, MT in the United States to Katowice in Poland – it could take two months for the parcel to arrive. If over the same period of time, the lovers split up by means of a text message or a Facetime call, the parcel will mark a time collapse in the media's ability to execute the lover's decisions. Lee MacKinnon (2016a) describes a similar case when she writes about her own break-up, which happened over the phone. The incident was followed by the arrival of a love letter, sent her way two weeks prior to the unexpected termination of the relationship. Lee explains this as the conflict of two discourse machines: the temporal and calculable machine of the analogue, and the ultra-rapid computational machine of the digital. This conflict places information exchange in two simultaneous orders: the older one which is literal/predigital and which Lee believes to be "probabilistic and determining"; and the recent computational/postdigital one "where temporal and spatial relations are expedited by digital processing" (MacKinnon, 2016a).

Those two orders make us think of human emotional relationships in terms of conflicted oppositions: analogue/digital, natural/artificial, fast/slow. At the same time, they carry within them a certain cultural and ethical value that causes a deceptive bias around our computational/postdigital practices of *amour*. We seem to see *slow* analogue *love* – one that develops steadily and is paced by the real time – as something more valuable, something more genuine than the love accelerated by technological means. But technology theorists advise against "lazy associations" which link "analogue systems with physics and nature, and digital systems with artifice and artificiality" (Bratton, 2016). A much more reliable perspective is one that presents the complexity of our experience as caused by the variety of physical realities. With respect to time, we may talk about a variety of dimensions (e.g. *online time*), institutions (e.g. *work time*), measurements (e.g. *calendar*) and agencies (e.g. *machine time*) that bring to a crisis our temporal notions and perceptions. The discovery that time is not linear, cyclical and successive, strains and challenges our operational efficiency. In comparison to machines (analogue or digital), we are not only operationally inadequate but also inflexible, which always leaves us behind the flow. Timothy S. Baker observes that interactions with and by means of technologies (either digital or analogue) are interactions "across multiple temporal rhythms" (Baker, 2012: 14). Our tempo and sense of time when blended with "machines" blend with the multitemporality of the machine-related media and devices: "a synchronous time of the software, the non-sequential time of the database, the time of the network and the time of the other users" (14). What we are dealing with is the obsolescence of human temporal capacities caused by "an alteration to the way we experience the occasions and events of our everyday lives, beyond a chronological sequence of events" (14).

Acceleration of feeling is an effect of the merging (or even accumulation) of multiple temporal realities. It is also a "victim" of the attempts to reconcile different "physical" paces. The shift of rhythms around love is not as much about a transition from analogue to digital – from slow to fast, from calculable to computational, from temporary to ultra-rapid – but about the buildup of a variety of temporal modes that rush our affective encounters and which dupe us into thinking that the speedup is objectively recent and exclusively related to digitization. Fast love is as much related to mobile texting as it is to telegraph messaging and pigeon post. They all reflect love's inherent tendency to overcome the "natural" rhythms of human exchanges as well as the biologic-ally conditioned haste for forming a "we" reflected in love's experience and expression. The temporal mechanics of love – by which I mean any form of affective companionship – rests on time-making (rather than living by time). Love does not ask "What is time?"; it asks: "How is time produced?" (cf. Baker, 2012: 2).

Loving Surveillance

The production of time situates love at the intersection of libidinal econ-omies (e.g. distribution of desire) and social industries (e.g. marriage), which operate by the "the [market] logic of exchange, accumulation, and profit" (Pettman, 2009: 26–27). The imperative of this situation is to compromise personal pleasure and social gain, which both want to happen fast, and both need "certainty" for success. Eva Illouz (2019) reminds us, as first observed by Niklas Luhman, that "certainty" stands in the center of social interactions; it reduces complexity in social processes and allows us to predict the outcomes of human relations. She also observes that, love

– along with truth, money, or power – is a medium of communication, helping create expectations, select one decision among many, connect motivation to action, and create certainty and predictability in relationships. Such media of communication create roles that in turn generate expected outcomes (to use Luhmann's example, a wife will not be rejected if she asks her husband "why are you home so late today?"). Predictability is a fundamental dimension of social interactions, to be found, for example, in rituals. When interactions are ritualized, they generate certainty about the actors' definition of a relationship, of their position in such relationship, and of the rules to conduct such relation. Certainty can be described as "refer[ring] to a person's ability to describe, predict, and explain behavior within social situations." (Illouz, 2019)

Predictable and codified, love rituals are all about certainty. Most of their efforts aim at eliminating risk to create "love without suffering" – a condition condemned by modern cultural critics (Badiou, 2012; Han, 2017; Horvat, 2016) and appreciated by "love amateurs." When pursuing affection, we want to make sure it works out. We also want to make sure it works out fast. As a primary ambition of romance (and other affective unions), a quick and successful match is encoded in human "biology" as much as it makes a fabric of the cultural practice of love. Despite the Biblical assurance that "love is patient," when it comes to romance, we tend to rush things, even structurally. Modern societies have devised a myriad of methods for accelerating romantic matches. Traditional matchmaking – especially the arrangement of unions by third parties, still popular and highly professionalized in many cultures – is nothing else but a technology for quick and low-risk coupling. A more recent and more liberated example of fast-love technology (no longer in service) was speed dating. Arranged as public events, speed dates ensured high exposure to a relatively high number of potential partners over several hours. Speed dating exploded in the 1980s as a response to the shrinkage of private time among young professionals. They took the form of quick face-to-face conversations during which the interviewees decided about the potential match. An important element of speed dates was information charts (a combination of a personal questionnaire and a chat protocol), used to help the daters assess their mutual compatibility. With respect to data collection and analysis, speed dates served as a solid prototype for match databases, now used in online dating for the quick estimation of chances. Although the predicted outcome of speed dating cannot compare to the outcome generated by today's algorithmic data-pools, it was certainly a step towards time-control and time-saving measures that still model romance effectiveness (Houser et al., 2008; Hollander and Turowetz, 2013).

When online dating took over in the 1990s, romantic profiling became the algorithms' job. This has not only increased romantic efficiency, but also improved the accuracy of romantic estimations with respect to speed/time. Debates around technologically managed relationships highlight two conflicts that stem from computational matching: on the one hand, digital profiling desocializes human encounters; on the other, it shows substantial effectiveness for real-life encounters. A study on the effectiveness of online dating for continued offline relations proves a strong and successful connection between online profiling and offline interactions (Sharabi and Dykstra-DeVette, 2019). There is a relatively quick and productive transition between the first dating platform contact, the first off-platform interaction (usually email messaging) and the first offline encounter (the final point of the matchmaking process). The same study elucidates our growing enthusiasm for algorithmic matchmaking: in other words, when it comes to a "mate choice," we seem to trust computers more than human (often our own) judgement.

An interesting thing about matchmaking algorithms is that they do not rely on preferences (at least not in preferences sensu stricto). What decides a successful pairing is the preferences variance, estimated by means of a number of factors that the algorithm learns to optimize. Criteria taken into account include attractiveness (first physical, then psychological, often measured by the attention we get from others in profile activity), choosiness (how much we swipe and consider options), competing desires (the so-called individual factor the algorithm learns from our activity) and social dynamics (according to Youyou et al., 2017, we tend to stick to people of a similar social and cultural profile, especially social class-wise). The algorithms most commonly used for match predictions are the Aspiration-Level Model (based on the value hierarchy of traits), the Kalick-Hamilton Model (taking attractiveness as a primary benchmark for pairing) and the Gale-Shapley Algorithm (using deferral for creating a stable match). A more recent example, the Resource Allocation Model (based on a technique of couple simulation by means of avatars), explores the traits of a person's potential and idealized partners by approximating the average, which is considered the best estimation of a solid match (Conroy-Beam, 2021). The way those algorithms work goes against traditional convictions about coupling. Two older arrangements: "likes attract likes" or "opposites attract" do not find reflection in the computational method we seem so much inclined to.

There is also a darker side to algorithmic pairing. Dating apps are notorious for reproducing wrong cultural models (such as gender bias, racial discrimination and patriarchal profiling). Old-fashioned and politically incorrect standards, granted by the media mechanics and acquired from the network environment (including media content), prevail in app dating systems (a good example might be matches between physically attractive, less educated and financially/professionally unstable women and more intelligent, often affluent men (Duportail, 2019)). Data extracted for algorithmic coupling exploit estimations of users' intelligence, situation, social status and cultural background. These, in turn, exploit the users' online behaviors (texting, posting, browsing and interacting online). The amplification of algorithmic bias gets extra support from the way the devices work. Swipe apps – observes Gregory Narr – are guilty of encouraging ignorance and disengaged discrimination. In his study on racial bias in online environments, Narr describes "swipe apps [as] a prototypical example of [algorithmic oppression]" responsible for promoting "protocols that foster absent-minded engagement." As he further explains, "[swipe apps] allow unconscious racial preferences to be expressed without troubling users' perceptions of themselves as non-racists. These preferences are then measured by recommender systems that treat 'attractiveness' as a zero-sum game" (2021: 219), another reminder that the design of media environments is still (over) dominated by rich white men.

And yet, we choose to rely on the apps. Our faith in algorithmically managed matches speaks through the statistics of internet dating services (Finkel et al., 2012). As of December 2015, OKCupid registered 1,804,993 signed-in users (1,493,205 of whom were American). A similar number of 1,804,933 users were registered the same year to eHarmony (Piskorski, 2014: 26). Lee MacKinnon defines this as a turn to "immediately quantifiable coordinates" (2016b: 163). Her own analysis of the use of GS (Gale-Shapely) matching algorithms stresses the growing trust in profiling protocols and satisfaction with the immediacy of the profiling process and match selection. She explains that

> [i]n the context of online dating platforms, the potential lover becomes a list of discrete *menus* – increasingly informational and calculable, considered in terms of *user's* ability *to control/command/alternate/delete*. Human attributes can be mapped on to the technical devices, whereby the potential partner is assembled according to techniques associated with digital processing: editing, construction choice, convenience, ubiquity, obsolescence, discretisation – features associated with digital technology and its protocols. Here, speed may be associated with the elision of meaningful translation between one and the other that can ameliorate desire only by eliding the threat of any gap with the immediacy of a new object or 'gadget.' (163)

Motivations behind this massive reliance on computationality with respect to love vary, but come in categories. A primary one seems to be our own disappointment with human reasoning, both cognitive and emotional. Frischmann and Selinger (2018) believe that there is a growing doubt in human decision-making skills with regard to rationality, objectives, productivity and gain. Since the advent of intelligent machines, our trust in "the sometimes slow, sometimes fast, error prone, easily distracted, and routinely distorted information process-ing by humans" gave in to the trust in *idealized intelligence* "that engages in rapid computation without errors in calculation, and more critically, without any systematic bias introduced by emotional distractions" (Oscar H. Gandy Jr. (2008) in Frischmann and Selinger, 2018: 192–193). At the same time, we believe machines to be more emotionally capable. It has become patently clear that many aspects of our emotional labor are being delegated to devices.

Another reason for our attraction to the computationality of romance are digital archives and geolocation media, which offer yet another immediate and comforting demystification of a potential partner. Collecting, sorting, combin-ing and otherwise processing information about a potential match or a significant other is an obsession related to either the efficiency-mania or a need to control the romance's trajectory. Surveillance is a new standard in romance. Although studies on Social Network Sites (SNS) and relationships pin surveillant behaviors to teenaged relationship styles, monitoring a partner is a universal occurrence. It is also universal knowledge that:

> in this day and age . . . everyone is stalking each other constantly. . . . it's this age of social media where people's information and pictures are so openly available that makes it just very tempting to want to know so many things about someone you don't know. (Frampton and Fox, 2018: 8)

Tokunaga (2011) defines interpersonal electronic surveillance (IES) as "surrep-titious strategies individuals use over communication technologies to gain awareness of another user's offline and/or online behaviors" (706). It is "a mindful and goal-oriented behavior" based on four characteristics of SNS: accessibility, multimediation, recordability, archival and geographical distance (706, 707). An important aspect of these characteristics is that they all rely on technologically enabled instantaneity, reflected especially in status stamps (e.g. "last seen"), geolocation apps or activity tracking (e.g. the visibility of likes and interactions on SNS). Surveillance affordances of SNS simulate the conditions of the IRL (in-real-time) access to, and insight into one's partner's whereabouts, activities and interactions. Research on retroactive jealousy points out that this temporal illusion generates many misconceptions about partners and leads to different forms of violence in relationships (e.g. Cohen et al., 2014). Common behaviors include different forms of infiltration. In a study conducted on a group of adolescents between the ages of sixteen and twenty-two, almost half of participants "had experienced having their romantic partners view their emails, social networking site messages, or their cell phone text messages without their permission." Other experiences included "having their romantic partner send messages via the Internet or mobile phone to control whom they spent time with and what they were doing" or "having their partner call or send them messages multiple times in a row "to control where they were or with whom they were together'" (Van Ouytsel et al., 2019).

SNS's surveillance is a way to keep up with the stages of a relationship (to know where we stand with the match or a partner) and to minimize the chances of failure (Thylstrup and Veel, 2018). Some strategies also aim at inciting trust and solidifying commitment (e.g. account access password sharing). Most certainly, they set up a new standard for a romantic dynamic: a new form of temporal togetherness. Of course, the monitoring of partners in relationships (for jealousy or other reasons) is as old as human loving relations. It is also not exclusive to romance, and has a history in other forms of loving bonds (friendship, parent-child relationships). With modern media, however, this strategy consolidates and routinizes what used to be an occasional occurrence. Technological surveillance is now a relationship routine based on the roles of "the observer" and "the observed," both of which are taken to the extreme by the instantaneous nature of modern-day social panopticons.

Disadvantages related to SNS's surveillance do not, however, discourage us from the use of fast media. The time-transcendence granted by hi-tech communication devices constantly wins us over, as it always has, especially when it comes to love. When the electrical telegram became common in the twentieth century, every third message dispatched by means of that media was a message of love or care (Bruton, 2015; Rosenkrantz, 2003). In her research on the role of hi-tech devices for romantic relationships, Sherry Turkle stresses the importance of *temporal control* that the new media introduced to contemporary flirting. She specifically highlights the new sense of sustainability (190) related, for instance, to the elimination of waiting ("They send an e-mail, and they expect something back fast," Turkle, 2011: 190, 166). Storey and McDonald (2014) draw the same conclusion with regard to texting. Many of their interviewees speak of a key role that texting has offered to time-control their romantic encounters. Their testimonials also stress a universal role of texting for the time-management of affectionate bonds.

> I think [texting] speeds things up more than anything, because now … you can constantly be in contact. … I think I'm closer to him because you get to know someone quicker 'cos you're texting them.
>
> (Storey and McDonald, 2014: 118–119)

Time-management motivations are also part of our proclivity for engaging with artificial subjects (a topic I have covered in Section 1). A participant in Sherry Turkle's study that I have already referenced confesses that there are a number of time-factors that are more beneficial in relationships with robots (or other technological entities) than with humans. Trust is one of them. He says: "You wouldn't have to know the robot, or you would get to know it much faster. . . . Human trust can take a long time to develop, while robot trust is as simple as choosing and testing a program" (2011, 71–72).

What is missing from this scenario is the machine's time, a perspective inaccessible to humans. Technological objects – in how they work – do not reflect human rhythms of living. Nor do they understand them or follow their trajectories. Technological objects have time of their own. They also have their own operational pacing, which, even though programmable and controlled by humans, is independent from the human time by virtue of its operational difference. Our interactions with technological devices are, therefore, organized by the collision of two temporalities: that of the machine and that of the human (MacKenzie, 2006). Both parties transact and negotiate in these interactions their own temporal affordances and capacities. In *Transductions. Bodies and Machines at Speed* (2006), Adrian MacKenzie explains that a machine's criteria of randomness and interactive engagement, with its systems of delays and accelerations, frustrate human interactiveness. For instance, for a machine to respond, it takes a "wait" for a click of the mouse or other steering mechanism (e.g. a keyboard). Conversely, machines' reactions to the steering commands surpass our systems of interactivness, which could never match the responsiveness of the machine (e.g. calculability). "A machine" – MacKenzie says – "works within a certain margin of indeterminacy maintained at its interfaces" (53). That assumes certain operational contingency, also in relation to time. "In preserving a margin of indeterminacy, technical artefacts, machines, or ensembles allow themselves to act transductively" (53). This is how they navigate and negotiate "repeated interactions between living and non-living bodies" (53).

What acceleration teaches us about our affectionate relations is that they do not happen in isolation but they are an outcome of different material realities (human/machinic, animate/inanimate, natural/human-made). Those realities operate at their own pace, and are often in conflict. Our affective relations resonate that conflict in how they deal with what feels like a transition from temporal and calculable to ultra-rapid modes of living. Interestingly, the latter is well inscribed into the "nature" of love. Preoccupied with efficiency, love cherishes haste. It also seeks solutions that quicken amorous endeavors and bridge empty gaps. It therefore adopts technologies able to accelerate the experience of togetherness. Those same technologies are believed to decelerate our desire, the faster we go through the possibilities of choice, encounters, options and variants that the love market lures us with today, the more drained we feel. The multitude of options we have in love do not seem to be the problem; the real problem is the tempo those options rotate in: how fast they come and go; how long they stay or last.

Frustrations we experience with regard to the accumulation of different times and tempos around our love practices reflect the general bewilderment we feel in the temporal make-up of living today. The most acute is the loss of temporal orientation on the one hand and the urge to find it on the other, both induced with an intensity that makes us aware of the irreversibility of our situation. According to Paul Virilio (1995), "with acceleration there is no more here and there, only the mental confusion of near and far, present and future, real and unreal . . ., a mix of history, stories and the hallucinatory utopia of communication technologies" (35). And yet, the confusion opens a new possibility: all of a sudden we start to realize that there is perhaps no "here and there," but a different temporal and spatial possibility yet to be explored. The realization is, however, not easy as we yield to the sense of conflict and contradiction (fast vs. slow) rather than the potential. As a result, we live in a paradox based on the ambition to rush desire in order to experience it slowly. This confuses the pleasures of love with achievements in love.

(Post) Script (Conclusion)

I am closing this book convinced that the debate I have deployed here exhausts only a fraction of what technoculture has created for the experience of loving. To write about love and technoculture is a pleasurable yet daunting task. It is also futile, all the more that technoculture is such a constantly evolving and ever growing environment, also in terms of capacity. Love, although more conservative in its proclivity for change (it is the same story relived forever), exhibits plasticity, which, when played out in a technocultural setting, unravels a new experiential potential. This is perhaps why love is so difficult to grasp and can be discussed only in fragments.

Problems I have critically addressed in this Element relate to experiences lived every day all across the globe. Hence, this Element is about anyone who has ever loved. This means many people and many different conditions of loving. To respect this multitude and variety, I have never been specific about what I mean by love. Just like I have not singled out any emotions as defining for this experience in technoculture.

The landscape of criticism and practice woven here aims to serve as a point of identification for all those experiences regarding love and technoculture we live by, and which we do not entirely comprehend. To extend the critical play of this identification, I finish this Element with a set of open-ended formulations, some of them contradictory, many of them personal. They gather the gist of the Element's endeavors as well as create space for new senses to emerge.

1. Love, the way we understand it, is its own circumstances (and the circumstances of meanings we ascribe to what we understand as love). It is thus impossible to speak of love in isolation, away from the circumstances, just as it is impossible to speak of cultures of feelings without situating them in the processes that condition human existence and habitat.

2. Technoculture shows that love – when experienced and practiced between people and in societies – is always a reflection of the human manner and practice. Discussions about changes in the way we love are in fact discussions about the changes in the human way and not in love itself. Love does not change – reflections do. They mutate in accordance with human pursuits after the augmented experiences of togetherness, in which love becomes subjected to practical transmutations.

3. As an ever-expanding experience, love is not some ontologically stable feeling or condition but a technology – a system of techniques complex in themselves – coordinated with other life technologies – artificial, and natural – that work together in order to create an intended effect.

4. We cannot therefore think of love as a victim of the increasing technologization. We may, however, think of love as an effect of systemic anthropomorphization, to which technologization is irrelevant, when looked at from the perspective of physical reality. The technosphere resonates with love's inherent endeavors to create the affect (feeling, emotion, intimacy). Togetherness – its formation and maintenance (the way we want to experience them) – evolves with technologies; and conversely, technologies evolve and advance alongside love's unrelenting need to overcome the natural capacities for the formation of a "we."

5. Ambiguous diagnoses around love and technology emerge from the conflicting dynamic between the experience of loving and the critical perceptions of love. Speaking of love always means speaking inside tautologies, paradoxes and conceptual abstractions. It also means speaking inside existing referents with which we describe reality. "Popular" binaries of natural/artificial, organic/technologized, animate/inanimate, tangible/intangible, IRL/virtual, online/offline, used for theorizing our experiences with the physically varied and multi-layered environment in particular flatten debates on the nature of loving. Love is more complex than our perspectives on it and therefore should be considered/imagined beyond the obsolete dilemmas of nature vs. culture. The "versus" paradigm is not sustainable with regard to love.

6. The assumption that love is endangered by technologies distorts the proper comprehension of love's modes and manners. It also distracts us from seeing through the human exploitative approach to the potential that love relations entail. Love is a great power. When appropriated by the logic of market economies, it loses its original function as a mode of existence and operates instead as a form of social contracts. This is what affective or emotional alienation means – to sacrifice one's affective states to affective transactions that corrupt the economies of desire.

7. The sense of intensity we experience in love today results from the old-age tendency to efficientize love. Another factor is the tendency to commodify love's potential. As the most desired state (situation), love is of a great value and therefore sells well. Market economies capitalize love-related emotions by adapting them to the market standards that see everything in terms of achievement, gain and win as contrasted with failure, loss and fluctuation of value.

8. Data is the currency of love associated with the transition of life to online reality. Data is the prevalent element of love discourse today. Our emotional transactions depend on the value and relevance of data that substitute and represent the actual bodies and personalities. Data is for affective labor what Bitcoin is for stock exchange. Or to put it differently: "love" data is Bitcoin for affective labor.

9. Technologies we use today – platforms, applications, add-ons, gadgets – should not be seen as new ways of loving. They are merely new incarnations of the old ways love has always followed and in which it has fulfilled its inherent desires. Therefore, we should see the new media in terms of new possibilities that technologies bring into play and which invigorate the old love scripts and scenarios. Technoculture is a condition for love understood as fabulations.

10. Augmentations experienced in late-modern affective encounters are an effect of the physical extremes that hi-tech put us under. Technological devices and human bodies represent different material qualities: different paces, different operational modes and thinking, different judgement of distance and space. Despite the common assumption that media are the extensions of human bodies and human relations (professional, social and private alike), it is humans who extend technologies today. We are witnessing a shift in the organization of environment wherein humans/people are as much inhabitants as they are infrastructures. This is what the shift from biosphere to technosphere means, the change in function with respect to auxiliarity.

11. Technocracies create environments where different material dynamics and different technics – those of humans and those of devices – clash with one

another. That means negotiations between different functions, capacities, objectives, temporalities: different logics (cognitive and emotional). This is what makes relationships with technologies so exhausting and yet so invigorating.

12. Love practices of late modernity show that we are surrounded by two kinds of bodies: organic bodies (e.g. human bodies) and media bodies, endowed with a variety of physical formats. Today's media – VR displays, wearable devices, mobile communication systems, stimulators, meters and others – as they gain embodiments achieve the status of the body.

13. The media we interact with are a point of contact between the bodies as well as an arena for physical (usually bodily) activities. They also incorporate a variety of properties and affordances – affective and physical alike – which induce in the users a state of affective presence. To say that media are sensitive is to say that they create a sensory (and sensual) environment in which human-machine interactions "trick" us into thinking that technologies we are dealing with can feel and receive feelings. The question to be answered yet is: if they indeed feel, what does the feeling actually mean?

14. The challenge of love interactions is the material properties of spaces in which we place love encounters. Virtuality, as representative of *new tangibility* – something that exists beyond concreteness – reconceptualises the traditional understanding of presence and place. Material associations impact the semantics of love, which in turn impacts our relationships. As the spaces we operate in lose traditional solidity, our relationships seem less concrete and less solid, which is a debilitating impression.

15. Technologies thrive on the energy of love as a semiotic system, which in turn exposes affection as a fundamentally constructed and imaginary condition. There is something strangely dehumanizing in technologies of togetherness, something that shows that when it comes to love, we perhaps have never been human.

References

Ackerman, J. M., Li, N. P. & Griskevicius, V. (2011). Let's get serious: communicating commitment in romantic relationships. *Journal of Personality and Social Psychology*, 100(6): 1079–1094.

Angerer, M.-L. (2015). *Desire After Affect*, New York: Rowman & Littlefield.

Badiou, A. (2012). *In Praise of Love*, London: Serpent's Tail.

Baker, T. S. (2012). *The Time and the Digital: Connecting Technology, Aesthetics, and a Process Philosophy of Time*, Hanover, NH: Dartmouth College Press.

Ballatore, A. & Natale, S. (2015). E-readers and the death of the book: or new media and the myth of disappearing medium. *New Media and Society*, 18 (10): 2379–2394.

Barrs, P. (2011). *The Erotic Engine. How Pornography Has Powered Mass Media Communication from Gutenberg to Google*, New York: Anchor Canada.

Barthes, R. (1990). *A Lover's Discourse. Fragments*, London: Vintage.

Bauman, Z. (2003). *Liquid Love. On The Frailty of Human Bonds*, Cambridge: Polity.

Bauman, Z. (2017). *Retrotopia*, Cambridge: Polity Press. [Kindle.]

Baym, N. K. (2010). *Personal Connections in the Digital Age*, Cambridge: Polity Press.

Ben-Ze'ev, A. (2008). *Love Online. Emotions on the Internet*, Cambridge: Cambridge University Press.

Bennett, J. (2010). *Vibrant Matter*, Durham: Duke University Press.

Berardi, F. B. (2017). Exhaustion. In I. Szeman, J. Wenzel & P. Yaeger, eds., *Fueling Culture. 101 Words for Energy and Environment*, New York: Fordham University Press, pp. 155–157.

Berlant, L. (2012). *Love/Desire*, New York: Punctum Books.

Best, S. (2019). Liquid love: Zygmunat Bauman's thesis on sex revisited. *Sexualities*, 22(7–8): 1094–1109.

Bode, L. M. (2005). From shadow citizens to teflon stars: cultural responses to the digital actor (unpublished PhD dissertation, University of South Wales).

Brabant, O. (2016). More than meets the eye: Toward a post-materialist model of consciousness. *Explore. The Journal of Science and Healing*, 12(5): 347–354.

Bratton, B. (2016). *The Stack. On Software and Sovereignty*, Cambridge, MA: MIT Press. [E-book.]

Breazeal, C. (2002). *Designing Social Robots*, Cambridge, MA: MIT Press.

Brown, B. (2010). Materiality. In W. J. T. Mitchell & M. B. N. Hansen, eds., *Critical Terms for Media Studies*. Chicago: University of Chicago Press, pp. 49–63.

Bruton, E. (2015). Love on the wire. *Viewpoint*, 106: 11.

Buckingham, D. (2011). Foreword. In M. Thomas, ed., *Deconstructing Digital Natives. Young People, Technology, and the New Literacies*, New York: Routledge, pp. ix–xi.

Capellanus, A. (1969). *The Art of Courtly Love*, New York: Norton.

Cashmore, E., Cleland, J. & Dixon, K. (2018). *Screen Society*, Cham: Palgrave Macmillan.

Castells, M. (1996). *The Rise of the Network Society*, London: Wiley-Blackwell.

Castells, M. (2009). *The Rise of the Network Society*, London: Wiley-Blackwell. [Kindle.]

Cavallaro, F. I., Morin, F. O., Garzo, A. et al. (2012). Growing older together. When a robot becomes the best ally for aging well. In J. C. Augusto, ed., *Handbook of Ambient Assisted Living*, International: IOS Press, pp. 834–851.

Cefai, S. & Couldry, N. (2017). Mediating the presence of others. Reconceptualizing co-presence as mediated intimacy. *European Journal of Cultural Studies*, 22(3): 1–18.

Christina, B. & Griffiths, T. (2016). *Algorithms to Live By. The Computer Science of Human Decisions*, London: William Collins.

Ciechanowski, L., Przegalińska, A., Magnuski, M. & Gloor, P. (2018), In the shades of the uncanny valley. An experimental study of human-chatbot interaction. *Future Generation Computer Systems*, 92: 539–548.

Cohen, E., Bowman, N. & Borchert, K. (2014). Understanding romantic jealousy responses to an ambiguous social network site message as a function of message access exclusivity. *Computers in Human Behavior*, 35: 535–541.

Comella, L. (2017). *Vibrator Nation. How Feminist Sex-Toy Stores Changed the Business of Pleasure*, Durham: Duke University Press.

Conroy-Beam, D. (2021). Couple simulation. A novel approach for evaluating models of human mate choice, *Personality and Social Psychology Review* 25 (3): 191–228, https://doi.org/10.1177/1088868320971258.

Cunningham, M. R. & Barbee, A. P. (2008). Prelude to a kiss: Nonverbal flirting, opening gambits, and other communication dynamics in the initiation of romantic relationships. In Sporecher, S., Wenzel, A. & Harvey, J. eds., *Handbook of Relationship Initiation*, New York: Psychology Press, New York, pp. 97–120,.

Dalesandro, C. (2018). Internet intimacy. Authenticity and longing in the relationship of millennial young adults. *Sociological Perspectives*, 61(4): 1–16, https://doi.org/10.1177/0731121417753381.

Deleuze, G. (1990). *The Logic of Sense*, London: The Athlone Press.

Duportail, J. (2019). *Amour sous l'algorithme*, Paris: Goutte d'Or.

Eco, U. (1994). *Reflections on the Name of the Rose*, London: Minerva.

Farman, J. (2012). *Mobile Interface Theory. Embodied Space and Locative Media*, New York: Routledge.

Faustino, M. J. (2018). Rebooting an old script by new means. Teledildonics – the technological return to the "coital imperative." *Sexuality & Culture*, 22: 243–257.

Finkel, E. J., Eastwick, P. W., Karney, B. R., Reis, H. T. & Sprecher, S. (2012). Online dating: a critical analysis from the perspective of psychological science. *Psychological Science in the Public Interest*, 13(1): 3–66.

Flusser, V. (2014). *Gestures*, Minneapolis: University of Minnesota Press.

Frischmann, B. & Selinger, E. (2018). *Re-Engineering Humanity*, Cambridge: Cambridge University Press.

Garcia, J. R., Reiber, Ch., Massey, S. G. & Merriwether, A. M. (2012). Sexual hookup culture: a review, *Review of General Psychology*, 16(2): 161–176.

Gatebox (2016). Gatebox – promotion movie. You Tube, www.youtube.com /watch?v=nkcKaNqfykg.

Goertzel, B. Mossbridge, J., Monroe, E., Hanson, D. & Yu, G. (2017). Loving AIL Humanoid Robots as Agents of Human Consciousness Expansion (summary of early research progress), 1–16. https://arxiv.org/abs/1709.07791.

Grace, L. D. (2020). *Love and Electronic Affection. A Design Primer*, New York: Taylor and Francis.

Green, L. (2002). *Communication, Technology and Society*, London: Sage.

Green, R. F. (1979). Troilus and the game of love. *The Chaucer Review*, 13(3): 201–220.

Guillén, B. (2017). Interview with Jonathan Rossiter. *BBVA Open Mind*, www .bbvaopenmind.com/en/technology/robotics/we-are-working-on-robots-that -can-reproduce-and-then-they-can-die/.

Guattari, F. & Rolnik, S. (2007). *Molecular Revolution in Brazil*, Los Angeles: Sexmiotexte.

Hall, E. T. (1966). *The Hidden Dimension*, New York: Anchor Books.

Han, B.-C. (2017). *The Agony of Eros*, Cambridge, MA: MIT Press.

Hollander, M. M. & Turowetz, J. (2013). "So, why did you decide to do this?" Soliciting and formulating motives for speed dating. *Discourse and Society*, 24(6): 701–724.

Horvat, S. (2016). *The Radicality of Love*, London: Polity.

Houser, M. L., Horan, S. M. & Furler, L. A. (2008). Dating in the fast lane. How communication predicts speed-dating success. *Journal of Social and Personal Relationships*, 25(5): 749–768.

Hui, Y. (2015). Towards a relational materialism. A reflection on language, relations and the digital. *Digital Culture and Society*, 1(1): 131–148.

Illouz, E. (2011). *Why Love Hurts. A Sociological Explanation*, Polity Press: Cambridge.

Illouz, E. (2019). *The End of Love. A Sociology of Negative Relations*, Oxford: Oxford University Press.

Janning, M., Gao, W. & Snyder, E. (2018). Constructing shared "space": Meaningfulness in long distance relationship communication formats. *Journal of Family Issues*, 39(5): 1281–1303, https://doi.org/10.1177/0192513X17698726.

Jenssen, B. P., Gray, N. J., Harvey, K., DiClemente, R. & Klein, J. D. (2014). Language and love. Generation Y comes of age online. *SAGE Open* 4(1): 1–8, https://doi.org/10.1177/2158244014525894.

Kaplan, L. J. (2006). *Cultures of Fetishism*, New York: Palgrave Macmillan.

Kaun, A. & Stiernsted, F. (2014). Facebook time. Technological and institutional affordances for media memories. *New Media and Society*, 16(7): 1154–1168.

Kolozsvari, O. (2015). Physically we are apart, mentally we are not. Creating a shared space and a sense of belonging in long-distance relationships. *Qualitative Sociology Review*, 11(4): 102–115.

Krzykawski, M. (2019). Eros i *techne*. Miłość w czasach automatyzacji. [Eros and techne. Love in the time of automatization] *Texty Drugie*, 5: 35–57.

Lagerkvist, A. (2015). The netlore of the infinite: death (and beyond) in the digital memory ecology. *New Review of Hypermedia and Multimedia*, 21(1/2): 185–195.

Lamont, E. (2017). "We can write the script ourselves". Queer challenges to heteronormative courtship practices. *Gender & Society*, 31(5): 624–646.

Lancel, K. & Maat, K. (website). E.E.G. Kiss. www.lancelmaat.nl/work/e.e.g-kiss/.

Lardellier, P. (2004). *Le Coeur NET, Célibat et amours sur le Web*, Paris: Belin.

Larsonneur, C., Regnauld, A., Cassou-Nogues, P. & Touiza, S. (2015). *Le Sujet Digital*, Dijon: Presses du Réel.

Lenhart, A., et al.(2011). Teens, cruelty and kindness on social network sites. Washington, DC: Pew Research Center.

Lepawsky, J. & Kyonghwan, P. (2006). Cyberspace. In S. Dasgupta, ed., *Encyclopedia of Virtual Communities and Technologies*, Hershey and London: Idea Group, pp. 110–112.

Levy, D. (2008). *Love + Sex with Robots. The Evolution of Human-Robot Relationships*, New York: Harper Perennial.

Levy, D. (2016). Why not marry a robot. In Cheok A. D., Delvin, K. & Levy, D., eds., *Love and Sex with Robots. Second International Conference, LRS 2016*,

London, UK, December 19-20, 2016, Revised Selected Papers, Cham: Springer, pp. 3–13.

Luhmann, N. (1986). *Love as Passion. The Codification of Intimacy*, Cambridge, MA: Harvard University Press.

Lyotard, J.-F. (1974). *Économie Libidinale*, Bloomington: Indiana University Press.

Ma, X., Hancock J. & Naaman, M. (2016). Anonymity, intimacy and self-disclosure in social media. *Proceedings of* CHI'16, May 7–12, 2016, San Jose, CA, USA, pp. 3857–3869, DOI: http://dx.doi.org/10.1145/2858036 .2858414.

Machulis, K. (2021). The proxemics of digital intimacy. In A. Malinowska & V. Peri, eds., *Data Dating. Love, Technology, Desire*, Bristol: Intellect, pp. 136–155.

McArthur, J. A. (2016). *Digital Proxemics. How Technology Shapes the Ways We Move*, New York: Peter Lang.

MacKenzie, A. (2006). *Transductions. Bodies and Machines at Speed*, London: Continuum.

MacKinnon, L. (2016a). Love machines and the Tinderbot bildungsroman. *E-flux*. https://www.e-flux.com/journal/74/59802/love-machines-and-the-tinder-bot-bildungsroman/.

MacKinnon, L. (2016b). Love's algorithm. The perfect parts for my machine. In L. Amoore & V. Piotukh, eds., *Algorithmic Life. Calculative Devices in the Age of Big Data*, New York: Routledge, pp. 161–175.

MacKinnon, L. (2018). Repeat after me: the automatic labour of love. *Journal of Aesthetics and Culture*, 10(3): 23–31.

MacKinnon, L. (2021). Romance in a time of dark data. In A. Malinowska & V. Peri, eds., *Data Dating. Love, Technology, Desire*, Bristol: Intellect, pp. 26–38.

MacKinnon, L., Thylstrup, N. B. & Veel, K. (2018). The techniques and aesthetics of love in the age of big data. *Journal of Aesthetics & Culture*, 10(3): 1–7.

Maines, R. P. (1989). Socially camouflaged technologies: the case of the electromagnetical vibrator. *IEEE Technology and Society Magazine*, June, 3–23.

Maines, R. P. (1999). *The Technology of Orgasm. "Hysteria," the Vibrator, and Women's Sexual Satisfaction*, Baltimore: The Johns Hopkins University Press.

Malinowska, A. (2018). The matter of kissing. In A. Malinowska & M. Gratzke, eds., *The Materiality of Love. Essays on Affection and Cultural Practice*, New York: Routledge, pp. 85–98.

Malinowska, A. (2019). Obiekty i technofilie [Objects and technofeelias]. *Texty Drugie*, 5: 18–34.

Malinowska, A. (2020). Sexbots and posthuman love. In K. Ross, ed., *International Encyclopedia of Gender, Media, and Communiation*, London: Wiley Blackwell (online).

Malinowska, A. (2021). Fast Love. Temporalities of Digitized Togetherness. In Malinowska, A. & Peri, V. *Data Dating. Love, Technology, Desire*, Bristol: Intellect, pp. 42–57.

Malinowska, A. & Miller, T. (2017). Sensitive media. *Open Cultural Studies*, 1: 660–665.

Marleau-Ponty, M. (1964). *The Primacy of Perception and Other Essays on Phenomenological Psychology, the Philosophy of Art, History and Politics*, Evanston, IL: Northwestern University Press.

Massumi, B. (2002). *Movement, Affect, Sensation. Parables for the Virtual*, Durham: Duke University Press.

Mayr, C. (2020). Symbolic vibration. A meaning-based framework for the study of vibrator consumption. *Journal of Consumer Culture*, 3(1): 1–19. DOI.10 .1177/1469540520926233.

Milgram, P. & Colquhoun, H. (1999). A taxonomy of real and virtual world display integration. In Y. Ohta & H. Tamura, eds., *Mixed Reality. Merging Real and Virtual Worlds*, New York: Springer, pp. 5–30.

Mori, M. (2012). The uncanny valley. *IEEE Robotics & Automation Magazine*, 19(2): 98–100.

Morozov, E. (2011). *The Net Delusion. The Dark Side of Internet Freedom*, New York: Penguin.

Mossbridge, J. & Goertzel, B. (2017). Designing an AI to love. Consciousness hacking. Ben Goertzel and Julia Mossbridge. www.youtube.com/watch? v=kQjOT_MLxhI.

Narr, G. (2021), The uncanny swipe. The return of a racist mode of algorithmic thought on dating apps. *Studies in Gender and Sexuality* 22(3): 219–236, https://doi.org/10.1080/15240657.2021.1961498.

Nozick, R. (1989). *The Examined Life. Philosophical Mediations*, New York: Simon & Schuster.

Öhman, C. (2020). A theory of temporal telepresence: Reconsidering the digital time collapse. *Time & Society*, 29(4): 1061–1081.

Papacharissi, Z. (2018). Introduction. In Z. Papacharissi, ed., *A Networked Self and Love*. New York: Routledge. [Kindle.]

Parisi, D. (2018). *Archaeologies of Touch. Interfacing with Haptics from Electricity to Computing*, Minneapolis: University of Minnesota Press.

Parisi, D. (2021). Virtual hugs and the crises of touch. In A. Malinowska and V. Peri, eds., *Data Dating. Love, Technology, Desire*, Bristol: Intellect, pp. 162–182.

Parisi, L. (2004). *Abstract Sex. Philosophy, Bio-Technology and the Mutations of Desire*, London: Continuum.

Paterson, M. (2007). *The Senses of Touch. Haptics, Affects and Technologies*, Oxford: Berg.

Patterson, S. (2015). Sexy, naughty, and lucky in love: Playing *Ragemon le Bon* in English gentry households. In S. Patterson, ed., *Games and Gaming in Medieval Literature*. New York: Palgrave Macmillan, pp. 79–104.

Perniola, M. (2017). *Sex Appeal of the Inorganic. Philosophies of Desire in the Modern World*, London: Bloomsbury.

Pettman, D. (2006). *Love and Other Technologies. Retrofitting Eros for the Information Age*, New York: Fordham University Press.

Pettman, D. (2009). Love in the time of Tamagotchi. *Theory, Culture & Society*, 26(2–3): 189–208.

Pettman, D. (2017a). *Creaturely Love. How Desire Makes Us More And Less Than Human*, Minneapolis: University of Minnesota Press.

Pettman, D. (2017b). *Sonic Intimacy. Voices, Species, Technics, or How to Listen to the World*, Stanford: Stanford University Press.

Pettman, D. (2018). Love materialism. Technologies of feeling in the 'post-material' world (an interview). In A. Malinowska and M. Gratzke, eds., *The Materiality of Love. Essays of Affection and Cultural Practice*, New York: Routledge, pp. 13–24.

Picard, R. W. (1995). Affective computing. *M.I.T Media Laboratory Perceptual Computing Section Technical Report No. 321*, 1–16.

Piskorski, M. J. (2014). *A Social Strategy. How We Profit from Social Media*, Cambridge, MA: MIT Press.

Ploeger, D. (website). Fetish. www.daniploeger.org/fetish0.

Ploeger, D. (2020). Interview, held on 20 November 2020.

Remagnino, P., Foresti, G. L., & Ellis, T. (2005). *Ambient Intelligence. A Novel Paradigm*, Boston: Springer.

Rheingold, H. (1992). *Virtual Reality. The Revolutionary Technology-Generated Artificial World and How It Promises to Transform Society*, New York: Simon & Schuster.

Richards, Riley (2016), 'Exploration of relational factors and the likelihood of a sexual robotic experience', in A. Cheok, K. Devlin and D. Levy (eds), *Love and Sex with Robots. Second International Conference, LSR 2016, London, UK, December 19–20, 2016. Revised Selected Papers*, Cham: Springer, pp. 97–103.

Rosa, H. (2015). *Social Acceleration: A New Theory of Modernity*, New York: Columbia University Press.

Rosenkrantz, L. (2003). *Telegram! Modern History as Told Through More than 400 Witty, Poignant, and Revealing Telegrams*, New York: H. Holt.

Sandvick, W. J., Hughes, J. W. & Atkinson, D. A. (1998). Method and device for interactive virtual control of sexual aids using digital computer networks. Google Patents. https://patents.google.com/patent/US6368268B1/en.

Schweizer, H. (2008). *On Waiting*, London: Routledge.

Sharabi, L. L. & Dykstra-DeVette, T. A. (2019). From first email to first date. Strategies for initiating relationships in online dating. *Journal of Social and Personal Relationships*, 36(11–12): 3389–3407, DOI: 10.1177 /0265407518822780.

Shaun, B. (2019). Liquid love: Zygmunt Bauman's thesis on sex revisited. *Sexualities*, 22(7–8), 1094–1109.

Shaviro, S. (2014). *The Universe of Things. On Speculative Realism*, Minneapolis: University of Minnesota Press.

Shaviro, S. (2016). *Discognition*, London: Repeater.

Shaw, D. B. (2008). *Technoculture: The Key Concepts*, Oxford: Berg.

Shopin, P. (2017). Algorithms we love by. Artificial intelligence may offer a playful way out of our stale thinking on romance. *Institute of Art and Idea Magazine* 71 (February 27), https://iai.tv/articles/algorithms-we-love-by-auid-1216.

Sigusch, V. (2008). *Geschichte der Sexualwissenschaft*, Frankfurt: Campus Verlag GmbH.

Simon, W. & Gagnon, J. H. (1986). Sexual scripts: Permanence and change. *Archives of Sexual Behavior*, 15: 97–120.

Sone, Y. (2014). Canted desire. Otaku performance in Japanese popular culture. *Cultural Studies Review*, 20: 196–222.

Sorokin, P. (1982). *The Ways and Power of Love. Types, Factors, and Techniques or Moral Transformation*, Philadelphia: Templeton Foundation Press.

Stenslie, S. (2014). Cybersex. In M. Grimshaw, ed., *The Oxford Handbook to Virtuality*. Oxford: Oxford University Press, pp. 303–322.

Stevens, J. (1979). *Music and Poetry in the Early Tudor Court*, Lincoln: University of Nebraska Press.

Stone, Y. (2014). Canted Desire. Otaku Performance in Japanese Popular Culture. *Cultural Studies Review*, 20(2): 196–222.

Storey, J. & McDonald, K. (2014). Love's best habit. The uses of media in romantic relationships. *International Journal of Cultural Studies*, 17(2): 113–125.

Strengers, Y. & Kennedy, J. (2020). *The Smart Wife. Why Siri, Alexa, and Other Smart Home Devices Need a Feminist Reboot*, Cambridge, MA: The MIT Press.

Strupp, H. H. (1955). An objective comparison of Rogerian and psychoanalytic techniques. *Journal of Consulting Psychology*, 19(1): 1–7.

Szczuka, Jessica M. and Kramer, Nicole C. (2016), 'Influences on the intention to buy a sex robot: An empirical study on influences of personality traits and personal characteristics on the intention to buy a sex robot', in A. Cheok, K Devlin, and D. Levy (eds), *Love and Sex with Robots. Second International Conference, LSR 2016, London, UK, December 19–20, 2016. Revised Selected Papers*, Cham: Springer, pp. 72–83.

Thompson, J.B. (1995). *Media and Modernity: A Social Theory of the Media*, Cambridge: Polity.

Thylstrup, N. B. & Veel, K. (2018). Geolocating the stranger: the mapping of uncertainty as a configuration of matching and warranting techniques in dating apps. *Journal of Aesthetics and Culture*, 10(3): 43–52.

Tokunaga, R. S. (2011). Social networking site or social surveillance site? Understanding the use of interpersonal electronic surveillance in romantic relationships. *Computers in Human Behavior*, 27: 705–713.

Toma, C. L. (2018). Connection, conflict, and communication technologies. How romantic couples use the media for relationship management. In Z. Papacharissi, ed., *A Networked Self and Love*, New York: Routledge. [Kindle.]

Turing, A. M. (1950). Computing Machinery and Intelligence, *Mind*, 236: 433–460.

Turkle, S. (2011). *Alone Together. Why We Expect More from Technology Than from Each Other*, Cambridge, MA: MIT Press.

Urry, J. (2008). Speeding up and slowing down. In H. Rosa & W. E. Sheureman, eds., *High Speed Society. Social Acceleration, Power and Modernity*, University Park: Penn State University Press, pp. 179–200.

Weizenbaum, J. (2021). ELIZA – A computer program for the study of natural language communication between man and Machine (1960). In Harry R. Lewis, ed., *Ideas That Created the Future*, Cambridge, MA: The MIT Press, pp. 271–288.

Woolley, B. (1992). *Virtual Worlds. A Journey in Hype and Hyperreality*, London: Penguin.

World Video Game Hall of Fame (2018). *A History of Video Games in 64 Objects*, Dey Street Books [Kindle.]

Van Ouytsel, J., Walrave, M., Ponnet, K., Willems, A-S. & Van Dam, M. (2019). Adolescents' perception of digital media's potential to elicit jealousy, conflict and monitoring within romantic relationships. *Cyberpsychology. Journal of Psychological Research on Cyberspace*, 13(3): article 3.

Virilio, P. (1995). *The Art of the Motor*, Minneapolis: Minnesota University Press.

Youyou, W., Stillwell, D. H., Schwartz A. & Kosinski, M. (2017). Birds of the feather do flock together: Behaviour-based personality-assessment method reveals personality similarity among couples and friends. *Psychological Science*, 28(3): 276–284.

Acknowledgements

This Element is an effect of five years of research that has been rehearsed in my multiple projects (including the National Science Centre OPUS grant no 2020/ 37/B/HS2/01455) as well as in a number of texts.

I dedicate this writing to my sons, Jakub and Igor who, as feeling digital natives and technology pundits, have been excellent interlocutors in the process of systematizing the Element's approaches.

Cambridge Elements⁼

Histories of Emotions and the Senses

Jan Plamper

University of Limerick

Jan Plamper is Professor of History at the University of Limerick. His publications include *The History of Emotions: An Introduction* (Oxford University Press, 2015); a multidisciplinary volume on fear; and articles on the sensory history of the Russian Revolution and on the history of soldiers' fears in World War One. He has also authored *The Stalin Cult: A Study in the Alchemy of Power* (Yale University Press, 2012) *and Das neue Wir: Warum Migration dazugehört. Eine andere Geschichte der Deutschen* (S. Fischer, 2019).

About the Series

Born of the emotional and sensory 'turns', *Elements in Histories of Emotions and the Senses* move one of the fastestgrowing interdisciplinary fields forward. The series is aimed at scholars across the humanities, social sciences, and life sciences, embracing insights from a diverse range of disciplines, from neuroscience to art history and economics. Chronologically and regionally broad, encompassing global, transnational, and deep history, it concerns such topics as affect theory, intersensoriality, embodiment, humananimal relations, and distributed cognition.

Cambridge Elements ≡

Histories of Emotions and the Senses

Elements in the Series

A full series listing is available at: www.cambridge.org/EHES

Printed in the United States
by Baker & Taylor Publisher Services